# The Mandela Effect:
## *Ascension*

BLUE BOODLE BOOKS

# The Mandela Effect:
## *Ascension*

By Roy Horne

# Copyright

Second Printing: 2016

ISBN 978-1-365-48206-9

Blue Boodle Books
236 Eskew Lane
Jessieville, AR 71949

www.meascension.com

# Dedication

*This book was written for and is dedicated to:*

*My sons: Levi & Tyler*
*&*
*My wife: Debbie*

# Contents

## Preface

I have written this book mainly for my two sons. I wanted them to have a record of what has happened to me, and indeed the world, in the last few years. As the reader, please keep in mind if I use the word 'you', I am not speaking to you personally. I am speaking to my sons though. So please remember my main objective when reading this book and do not take offense.

I wrote this book rather hurriedly, I felt it important. I did not give a hoot about fragmented sentences. I wrote the way I talk. I apologize to all English Teachers.

Also, if you are someone who is very rigid about their beliefs, any belief, this book may not be for you.

Roy Horne
September 20, 2016

# Part One:

*Ascension*

*Hopi Mask*
*Wall Art Painted By Collin Thompson*
*monothompson@gmail.com*

The Mandela Effect is so named because of a unique worldwide phenomenon that continues today, and will presumably forever. When Nelson Mandela died December 5, 2013, there were many people who became somewhat confused. It seems this whole group of people from different parts of the world had the same memory of Mandela dying in 1983. I am one of these people. Instead of being free of prison and becoming president of South Africa, we remember Mandela dying in prison. We remember the riots that took place and especially we remember quite vividly the funeral.

But it did not stop there. The notorious floodgates were opened and eventually hundreds and hundreds of memories from one group did not match the memories of the other group. And within these two groups were subgroups that had 90% the same memory. It is so strange because I am really talking about the collective consciousness of the groups and the whole. I found it very intriguing. I remember that in the late nineties there was some talk about people reappearing after being dead for some time. I took it to be an Elvis sighting. A small group of people that had different memories than the public at large claimed parallel realities were to blame. They claimed to be aware at a different level than, well the unaware, which would be everybody but them. I remember reading how they claimed they could access parallel realities and were able to use this gift for healing. I do not remember if they were able to or not.

Somewhere in the middle of 2015 I found myself in the hospital. I was just shy of 65 years old and had never been in a hospital in my life. I had been working some long hours, but most of those hours were driving and that had never bothered me. I found myself doing some very strange things. It wasn't like dementia or anything, I knew what I was doing at the time and must have had a reason.

However somewhere in the middle of the process, the flow continued without my input and I found myself confused, relegated to a non-participant. It was like going into the kitchen to get a glass of water. You suddenly look at the glass in your hand, and while you are wondering, where did that come from, someone fills it with water. And you – are – the – only – one - there.

One morning my wife had to call for an ambulance. It seems that if you asked me I could not have given you my social security number. It was more than just a feeling of confusion; it was like a very intense anxiety attack. I can only suppose because I am not prone to anxiety. Something was going on and I felt out of control.

Even with all of the tests that the insurance company would pay for, the physicians could not really find anything definite. My blood pressure seemed to be slightly elevated and my heart slightly enlarged, but hell, I was 64 years old. They prescribed medication, which I tried, but it didn't seem to do any good, so I quit.

Fast forward a year and I find myself looking into the flat earth theory. Crazy, right? Everyone knows the earth is round! Well, I don't know. And this is very important to me. Not that the earth is round or flat, but important that I make a decision based on my own research. Why doesn't everyone do that? If you believe the earth is round, what is your basis? Do you believe that because there was a globe in every classroom you had as a youngster? There is so much modern scientific evidence, if you just open your mind, that the view we have of earth from space by NASA is fake. There are only two images and they don't even match each other. A Japanese satellite recorded the earth's rotation for twenty five hours. You can find that online also. However in the entire twenty five hours the cloud formations never moved. Very strange, wouldn't you say?

The flat earth folks can prove that the earth is not what we are told. There are hundreds of examples on the internet in which people can see ships or city landscapes from a 50 mile distance. I don't know how many you can find of the Chicago skyline across Lake Michigan alone. There were so many that the nightly news in Chicago reported that it was a mirage. That

is impossible with the supposed curvature of the earth. And no person has come forward that can prove the flat earth people wrong. And they have a pretty impressive line up of pilots, ballistic missile design engineers, aircraft instrumentation design engineers, and of all things, railroad engineers.

I pulled up several documents on the construction of railroad lines all over the world. (Yes, I do that kind of thing.) I looked at calculations galore. If you know how a railroad works you know you have to have fairly flat terrain. That is why they tunnel and bridge everywhere. Engines do not like to pull uphill with such heavy loads. It really is amazing. No calculations at all involving the curvature of the earth, in fact quite the opposite. And amazingly enough a large percentage of the structural engineers made an effort to point that out!

They had to layout, completely, the topography of a rail line for hundreds of miles. They had to determine how much dirt would have to be moved or filled, how many bridges or tunnels would have to be constructed. In a one hundred mile long perfectly flat line there is a difference in elevation of 666.667 feet, *if* the earth is the 24,901 mile circumference globe that we are told. (Number of miles squared multiplied by eight inches, divide by twelve for feet.) No matter how hard you try and rationalize it otherwise, that fact has to be part of any calculation.

Add to that the amazing line up of physicists, including Einstein, that have concluded that there is no known way to know if the earth is spinning or not. What does that mean? Well, if you hold to the heliocentric model, then the earth spins at 1,040 miles per hour around the sun. If you hold to the geocentric model, than the earth is stationary and the universe is spinning around. Either way, where is the point where the earth's atmosphere, spinning or stationary, meets space? That should be a very recognizable point.

If the earth is spinning then a helicopter could simply hover and cover 1,000 miles in an hour. *"Oh no it can't Roy; the atmosphere has to be spinning also"*. I can't find the proof. I can't find the exact proof of what this earth really looks like. Have you ever wondered why there has never been a North to South circumnavigation of the earth? Or there never had been where I came from. I have no desire to check this planet's history. I suspect that the South Pole is not what it appears to be.

I have come to lean toward the beliefs of Nikola Tesla. Tesla did not believe that the earth was a planet. He believed the earth was an electromagnetic environment with no edges! I have no proof. I don't know. But Tesla was an amazing man. He claimed, just like Wernher Von Braun, that his information was from the 'other side.' Most of his work has been confiscated by the United States Government. There is no telling what Tesla might have discovered and, left to his own devices, would have brought to mankind. However Westinghouse was very greedy and destroyed Tesla who died impoverished. You see Tesla knew that energy was free for the taking. Tesla knew that everything was vibration and energy.

I kept finding the flat earth information tied with the Mandela Effect. I knew nothing of the world-wide phenomenon. It did not take long for me to realize that the world I knew was gone and I was living in a very similar but different timeline.

The first change I remember was a company logo. JCPenny was now JCPenney. Now, I know in my former world how that company spelled its name. My sister even worked at the JCPenny store at North Park Mall in Dallas. It just did not make sense. A company might change a logo, but not a name. Or would they? Oscar Meyer was now Oscar Mayer. That cracked me up. Everybody knows the

6

Oscar Meyer Weiner song; my bologna's second name was M.*E*.Y.E.R.

And what about Ford? The Ford logo now had a squiggly pig's tail on the F. I looked online and found that the Ford logo has been the way it is today since 1912. Really? I know the Ford logo. I have owned several Fords. My father owned several Fords. This was not a memory problem. I looked at other vehicle logos and found that Volvo, Volkswagen, and Chevrolet's were different. And according to company history the logos of these companies had not made a change, ever.

And there are hundreds and hundreds more. It is so, so strange. And the strangest thing is that I know more people are experiencing the effect and refuse to believe or just have not really noticed anything different at all. There is fear in the eyes of the beholder. And then they check out. The rational mind will force them to say things like, *"Do you realize what you are asking me to believe?"* or *"I can't wrap my brain around what you are saying."* And then they are comfortably back in their reality and go home and tell their wife, *"Ol' Roy Boy has finally lost it. Always knew he would eventually!"*

It was all getting too weird. Berenstein Bears was now Berenst*a*in Bears, Febreeze was now Febreze, Bragg's Apple cider vinegar was now Bragg, Kit-Kat Bar was now KitKat, The dash in Coca-Cola was gone, replace with an elevated dot. All different. And some do not make any sense. For instance Cup O' Soup is now Cup Soup. What is that, Cup Soup? I was in Wal-Mart the other day and the sign down one grocery isle proudly says Cup O' Soup, but the product on the isle is Cup Soup. I got a good chuckle over that.

Some names went back to my childhood memories. Do you remember Jiffy Peanut Butter? Well Jiff Peanut Butter has existed on this planet since 1958 and Jiffy has never existed. Do you remember Cracker Jacks? Sure you do! Well apparently the Cracker Jack brand has been a household brand name for over 120 years, according to their website. How about this, do you remember Fruit Loops. Well now it is Froot Loops. Do you remember Looney Toons? Well get this, now it is Looney Tunes! It's Toon's man, like you know, cartoons. What is Tunes anyway? It wasn't about any musical tune!

Do you remember the old joke, What do you give your ninety year old grand father for his birthday? Depends! Get it, Depends. Depends is/was an adult incontinence product. Now it is Depend. Now the joke makes no sense.

And then I started noticing the pop culture changes. Star Wars Luke, I'm your father, became No, I'm your father. Now that ain't right. I know that line. Barbara Streisand is now *Barbra.* I owned an album of her's that was simply entitled Barbara. Pete Townsend of the rock group, *Who*, is now Pete *Townshend*. Sally Fields is now *Sally Field* and her famous Oscar acceptance speech is changed. Charles Schultz of Peanuts fame is now *Charles Schutz*.

8

Do you remember the Queen song *We Are the Champions?* Do you remember it ending this way: *We are the champions.....of the world!* Well apparently in this reality those last words were never sung.

Life is like a box of chocolates became life *was* like a box of chocolates. It's a wonderful day in the neighborhood became *this* neighborhood. An Interview with A Vampire became *The* Vampire. And if I pointed this out to anyone they would just give me a strange look. And my wife, bless her heart, she remembers the earth I remember. And I would be just way out there on this amazing, once in the history of man event, and I would be amazed that she was not as hyped up as I was. And I would say*," Don't you understand what has happened? This is not our world!"*

*"I know,"* she would say, *"But what are you going to do about it?"* That is so very unlike her to be so nonchalant.

I was on the internet looking at all the changes, (*"You've just been on that internet too much Roy*!" I keep hearing that running through my head. But it is not my voice. I hear a real old woman sitting on a front porch way out in the mountains somewhere. She leans over and spits and says,*"You've been on that galdarn internet too much if you ask me*!") I was totally fascinated with this remarkable turn of events. I found some people arguing online, (not hard to find), about the JFK assassination. It seems in this time line that Gov. Connally was riding in a middle seat with his wife. The front seat had a driver and a Secret Service man riding shotgun. Well, not where I came from. The car only had two seats not three. Connally rode shotgun and his wife was not involved.

Now you may say, well you are getting old and really don't remember. I tell you there are things that I know, and I know that I know them. And this is one. Kennedy was killed November 1963 in Dallas. One year later my family moved from Arkansas to Dallas. I was very intrigued with the whole affair for some reason. And I am sure there were only 4 people in that limo and not 6. There is still online evidence to verify this. There is a Life Magazine story with a photo of an exact replica of the limo. And that photo was taken at the Henry Ford Museum. And Ford made the limo. And it only has two seats. Crazy right! This finding of evidence of a similar but not exact world to this is being called residual evidence. You can find evidence online in old newspaper ads and magazines that match the memories of the Mandela group.

Well, crazy did not stop there. The damn human anatomy changed. The rib cage is not the same. There is an extra rib in the back and the front is either connected or much closer to being connected to the sternum. The shoulders are much straighter with no slope. The stomach is higher and to the left; which moved the heart more central. The skull is different with eye sockets, brow line, and temple area different. The current brow line is broader and more pronounced and there is a small indent just

10

above each temple area that runs straight back. The skull here looks rather blocky to me. But the eyes are the real deal. It is for some reason very unsettling to me. I don't know why, but just spooky. If you look at the eye socket from a skull from this planet you would see deeper sockets and in the center you would see slots that look like this: / \. In the skull I remember there was a small round hole, or slots that ran the opposite direction and were much, much smaller than the ones here on this earth. Everything is just a little different.

Every day there was more on the internet. Now if you are not going through this you won't understand. If you are, well you know this is the damnest thing! This is better than science fiction. This is amazing and you can not help but want more information. And there is a lot of information, good and bad, on the internet. But that's cool.

I found a lot of people were talking about the location of South America. So I looked that up online and what do you know! South America is about 1500 miles too far east. Chile used to line up north and south with the state of Texas. And why is the southern part of Chile crumbling all apart? Wait a minute! I looked at a globe. Then not believing my eyes and knowing how globes can be, I pulled up world maps online. And what do you know. The Earth's geography changed.

There is now no land mass at the North Pole. Really? I remember how hard it was to get to that particular point of the world. But it was done several times and the first successful ones used dogs and sleds. Well, I was so surprised to see that on this planet you can go to the North Pole anytime you might want to. You just take a huge old ice cutter and chop your way in. Here, on this planet, the North Pole sits at some theoretical position in the Artic Ocean. They sell cruise packages to the North Pole!

Greenland is huge and instead of being an independent country, it is part of Denmark. Australia is way too far North and no longer the land from down under. North and South Korea moved from the familiar spot near Vietnam and are now located far North just off the coast of Japan. Midway Island is now part of the Hawaiian chain of islands, and that makes no sense. I remember Midway being about half way between Hawaii and the Philippines. It was crucial in WWII for an air field for bombing runs and supplies. (That would not be necessary with Australia in its present position and I assume that is exactly what happened. I assume because I don't know. I have not investigated WWII on this planet and do not intend to. I do not have time to learn another world history.) China is way too small. Russia has a peninsula on its east coast. Alaska is at least three times larger than where I came from. I became aware that I am a stranger in a strange land. This is not my home.

And then the stars I look at every night told me something was not right. I went online and looked up Earth's location in the Milky Way. And what do you know! This is not where I came from! Where are my stars?

I came from an Earth that was way out on the outer reaches of the Milky Way, out on the end of a long arm known as the Sagittarius Arm. This Earth is located directly across the center of the Milky Way and on a small stub of an arm called the Orion Arm. This is not my Earth!

But the changes that really set me off, and exposed how unknowingly legalistic I had become, was all of the changes in the King James Bible.

I live in a small community in rural Arkansas. I was active in a small Baptist church for over 20 years. During that time I wore many hats. At one time I was Sunday School Director, Advanced Bible Class instructor, Faith leader, sound tech, and I led the Wednesday night Bible class for one and a half years while we searched for a new pastor.

To properly teach the advanced Bible class I had to use the King James Version of the Bible combined with a Strong's Concordance. I am very familiar with the King James Bible. It is, or was, my favorite version. So when I discovered that certain versus in the KJV had changed, I was more than upset. All of the changes seemed so sinister to me. They were not random. There seemed to be some agenda at work.

I won't go into all of the changes at this time, mainly because I know I would have to go into too much detail as to how the meaning has changed and now makes no sense. However, I found words like matrix instead of womb, bottles instead of wineskins, and penny instead of denarius. And

words that I have never seen in any Bible before
like: unicorn, piss, pilot, plane, pavement, India,
Spain, Italy, countries instead of nations, president,
and more and more.

And entire phrases had changed and with some evil
tint. The Lion shall lay with the Lamb is now the
wolf shall dwell with the lamb. No meaning there.
The verse is not about a new Earth in which all the
little animals will get along. It is about the finished
product Earth, Kingdom of Jesus, the Lion of Judah,
the Lamb of God. And in the middle of the Ten
Commandments no less God says He is called
Jealous, with a capital "J". If that had been so in my
neighborhood there would have been the Holy
Name of Jealous churches on every street corner.

And my Lord, why in the world does the Bible now
say in the Old Testament that God, knowing how
the Israelites had a lust for flesh, gave his
permission for the eating of flesh and the drinking
of blood. Deuteronomy 12:20: *When the Lord thy
God shall enlarge thy border, as he hath promised
thee, and thou shalt say, I shall eat flesh, because
thy soul longest to eat flesh; thou mayest eat flesh,
whatsoever thy soul lusteth after.*

Ezekiel 39:17: *And, thou son of man, thus saith the
Lord God; Speak unto every feathered fowl, and to
every beast of the field, Assemble* (notice the capital
A after the comma. There are errors all over the
place now) *yourselves and come; gather yourselves
on every side to my sacrifice that I do sacrifice for
you, even a great sacrifice upon the mountains of
Israel, that ye may eat flesh and drink blood.*

14

Eat flesh and drink blood! There is an evil intent all throughout the Bible now. It is disheartening. And every single mature Christian I have asked the question: Who will lie with the Lamb? And all of them, except the pastor, have answered Lion. Every single mature Christian I have asked the question: Do not put new wine into what? And all of them, except the pastor, have answered skins or wineskins. (I am not picking on the pastor. I don't think that it is his fault. I will get into that later.) And every single mature Christian I have asked to recite the Lord's Prayer has recited what I know to be the Lord's Prayer from Matthew. The key words being: *Forgive us our trespasses as we forgive those that trespass against us.* One hundred percent, every single one, have answered the same way. If you are reading this and you remember hearing or perhaps even using that phrase in the Lord's Prayer, then you are not from here. In this present timeline that particular version never existed.

I became a watchman on the wall. My hands were up in the air. How could we work or play at a time such as this? Why will not anyone listen to me? Satan has changed the Bible and we are under attack! I was the watchman on the wall, it was midnight, the enemy was at the gate, I had sounded the alarm, and everyone rolled over and went back to sleep like it was a vacation Saturday morning.

I contacted two men that graduated from high school with me. Both are now preachers. I sent them email warnings. I received generic replies about there being so many translations today that one could get confused. I shot back telling them that every King James Bible on the planet, including the original 1611, had been changed over night. I have not heard from them since. I am not blaming these good men. What are they supposed to do? They handled it the best they knew how. But someday someone in their congregation that still clings to the old KJV will raise their hand and ask why Easter is in Acts Chapter 2 instead of the word Passover.

I called a very good friend that is a preacher. I read the passages to him and he agreed that those words were definitely not the words he remembered in his Bible. He was on the same page with me for a short term. Then he just could not come to terms with changes to God's Word. He kept clinging to the belief that the Bible is the infallible Word of God and could not be changed. Herein lays the big problem. The Word of God is Jesus. The book called the Bible is an artifact that has been tampered with by man for centuries.

I called a friend that pastors a church in South Dakota. He listened to me on the phone and promised to get back in touch. I have not heard from him since. All in all I went to three deacons and six pastors. I finally figured out that they each in turn called my pastor and most have been giving me plenty of room. I am sure they are doing all they know to do in this strange situation.

I was beside myself. All of these changes and now the Bible! I called my Pastor and told him what was going on with the Bible. His exact words to me, *"Look Roy, I know you believe the Earth is flat. I don't have time for this.*" He did take the time to come to my workplace later that day to apologize for sounding condescending. He is a good man. He promised me he would look into the changes and get back to me. He never did.

After a week of waiting on the preacher to call back I decided to approach another deacon. I called him and he said he was busy that day but would look into things. I guess he called the preacher that night because I called him the next day and his exact words to me were, *"Roy I don't have time for this."*

That was enough! I went directly to the church and walked into the pastor's office with my KJV opened to Acts Chapter 2 and my finger on the word Easter. We went back and forth with the word Easter, piss, and unicorn for God's sake. He told me he remembered as a child in church laughing when the preacher read, *pisseth* upon the wall. He had no way of knowing that I had just had a conversation with my neighbor who is our oldest deacon and we both laughed that if *pisseth* had ever been in the Bible we would have been in trouble for snickering in church!

I told him if it was just me seeing these changes I would be worried, but there were thousands, maybe millions of us experiencing the same effect. I will never forget his all too human rational response. It angered me at the time but now I find it hilarious. I am not laughing at the preacher, I am laughing at our human condition. He said this," *But you can't prove the Bible has changed because you have no Bible showing otherwise. And even if the number of*

17

*people you claim seeing the same thing is in the millions, with over 7 billion people on the earth that would be a small and insignificant number."* What percentage of people on Earth do we have to have to qualify as an actual occurrence?

And then the realization came upon me that his Bible had not changed! He was from this timeline and this Earth. I know I came off crazy trying to apologize, me being from a different planet and all. *Wait a minute; you are not from this planet?* He asked. I was not helping my case. I left the church house.

What really was amazing to me was that I could not find anyone who knew enough about geography, world history, or the King James Bible to give me a definitive answer on anything. It was like being on Jay Leno's Man on the Street!

It took a couple of more hours for all the rest of the city of man thinking to burn out. My mind was struggling. And then *POP!* I let go and I stopped the world!

# Part Two:

## *Toltec*

*Chac mool*

I was introduced by chance, sometime in the early part of 1971, to a few people who lived outside of Austin, Texas. It was the most fortunate meeting of my life. I did not know it at the time. These people were very adept with peyote. They felt peyote was put here as a gift. If treated as a living being it can be taken to remind beings that they are made of energy and light. These lanky guys that grew compost and worms for a living did peyote ceremoniously. They were enlightened and it was exciting.

The first four or five times I did peyote was with these two organic farmers. The effects of those times and the many times for the next eighteen months were mind expanding. It is a natural thing. I have never considered these plants to be deadly or dangerous, they are spiritual in nature. They are the link to understanding what nature is saying to us. It is as if nature is communicating all the time, and what we are seeing in nature is the *manifestation of nature's intent*. And if you want to visit the *field of probability* of nature's intent you have to go on an excursion. Three times in that year and a half I did three day excursions.

A three day excursions was a pretty messy affair. You had to have some people to take care of you. You start off one night around nine o'clock by ingesting four to six fresh mature peyote buttons. The buttons are prepared by removing the white center and every white vein that runs from the middle white part to the top of the button. This white substance is not good. Many people think the white part is strychnine, but that is not so. The buttons are blended in a banana smoothie. After the first dose you take two or three buttons every six to eight hours for the entire seventy two hour period. I have witnessed many marvelous things during those times and have had conversations with very real beings that exist on our plane of consciousness but vibrate at such a high rate that we do not notice them. That is what they told me anyway.

The essence of what is learned is invaluable. You basically learn that everything is light and light is information. All information flowing continuously is true communication from your soul and is directed at your heart, not your mind. However this communication is filtered through the mind and is the reason that the world is as you see it today. That flow of real communication has been replaced by programmed belief structures that, being fear based, keep the natural vibration field from being accessed. And this has resulted in a collective consciousness that is out of tune with the very frequency of the Earth. It is about harmony and dissonance.

If you can, picture a movie theatre and each person in the audience has his own projector. Everyone is projecting on the screen and everyone sees his own movie. It is living within the collective consciousness. The problem arises in that each person projecting thinks on some level that they are the star of the movie on the screen! This is the world of men. Something is surrounding us on another level at all times that most people are simply unaware of. It is the energetic world. The little soul simply processes out anything that does not fit in the rational world. However, the communication on that energetic level is very valid and real.

Plants have for thousands of years opened man's consciousness potential and revealed to man his energetic reality and his connection to God. For thousands and thousands of years these plants have been used for a specific purpose, to communicate spiritually with God. I know it seems a stretch, but it is a very spiritual affair. Or it was for me. I am sure there are many who are just after a joy ride. But doing a three day excursion is not a joy ride.

The worm farmers taught me about the Toltecs and peyote showed me the other side of reality. This ancient knowledge of dual reality has been known throughout Central America for thousands of years. And really it has been known and utilized by all the indigenous peoples throughout the world. A young tribesman stayed in his mother's care until a certain age. As a youngster he learned the social culture necessary to fit in and be productive within the tribe. As soon as he reached the age of accountability the elder men of the tribe would take the young man and *open up his head*. Young men for thousands of years have been shown other realities through the use of plants. With the proper guidance this expansion of the mind produces a spiritual warrior.

I am of the opinion that everything we know about navigating society we have learned in the third grade on the playground. In the third grade you were being bullied, doing the bullying, or more than likely just unaware of the real world. Every dynamic that you use in business, family, church,

22

whatever the social junction, you learned in the third grade on the playground.

The problem with society is that custom hinders progression in some areas. We as a society have not, and probably never will, progress past the dynamics of the third grade see-saw. This is like the young man and his teaching from his mother. We are not shown the other side, the real spiritual side. We should be, as the young tribesman was, not only shown the other side, but encouraged and guided to be able to navigate and utilize the other side. It is easier than you think, once you have seen the other side.

All culture, ancient or modern, is confining to free man. All cultures have rigid boundaries that are set within a specific belief system. It was the same thousands of years ago. It seems that we are unable to learn a lesson. We are more than this material reality; we actually *create* this material reality! Stopping the world that you are making breaks the boundaries of culture. And the breaking of the boundaries of culture results in isolation from society. And that is why the shaman always was a mysterious and secretive person.

The knowledge that the shaman relied upon was handed down to him by his benefactor. And a shaman would hand his knowledge down to an initiate or apprentice. I think it is important that you do not let these terms influence you at this time. It was kept mysterious and magical and all kinds of names were given to people, objects, and ceremonies to keep the uninitiated away. And really what it amounts to is opening a new and separate reality and, through *intent and will*, making this reality as real as the material reality we live in every day. It is faith in action.

This feat of creating another reality finally leads a person to the realization that the reality that is being searched for is the reality that you have always lived in, hidden from you at arms length, and the reality you thought you were living in is just a facade, all vapor, and not real. What a jolt! And this is what these plants show you from day one. These plants destroy the boundaries of culture and wrap the material world reality around your *intent.* I was shown the reality of the present cultural paradigm grid of control and once shown that you can never go back. From that time I have only wanted to be free. I chose a path with heart. I tried to learn the way of following your heart and calming the racket in your head. Or, to be more accurate, a path with heart chose me. And this type of path goes back thousands of years to the Olmec, Toltec, Mayan, Aztec, Navaho, Hopi, and even the Egyptians. I do not know why, it just rang true in my heart.

The indigenous people of the America's supposedly came over the Siberian land bridge after the last ice age. These ancient people moved south and became the Hopi, Olmec, Toltec, Aztec, Mayan, and the others. There is evidence that these people made it as far as a high mesa in Chile. This procession took thousands of years. There is evidence in the form of some type of language that ties these exact people in Chile to a people that lived many thousands of years ago in Utah.

The Olmec were from Southern Mexico and were known as the recorders of time. They lived over 15,000 years ago. These were ancient men of knowledge that started the process of keeping time as it related to the coming and going of the Earth Ages. But more importantly, they are the ones who set time in motion, the dawning of self-awareness and consciousness. According to their legends we are living in the 4th age. The coming 5th age will be the last. Three other times civilization has reached a very sophisticated level only to be destroyed and sent back into the stone ages. The Olmec were devoted to setting a clock and calendar that would place this timeline specifically. It took them over one thousand years to make those calculations. These were the Ancient Men of Time.

From the Olmec came the Toltec. The Toltec were not so much a single tribe of people as they were a group of artist. They specialized in all kinds of art and craft and in particular the Art of Living. They were great builders of things. After the Olmec calculated the point of entering this age, the Toltec built upon the concept of ages utilizing a very unique and sophisticated calendar. This calendar is the basis for the Mayan and Aztec calendars.

The Toltec recognized that everything is vibration and light. The light from Source transmits all information from the "IS". It really is a wonderful system. The light from Source travels through the Soul and into the many manifestations of the Soul.

We are like mirrors. We reflect the light from Soul and that manifests, through us, as the reality we live in. The ancient man saw his energetic surroundings and interpreted with a different type of perception than we use today. When things were not right with his hunting or some other life action he first looked within. The problem with the hunting might not be a nature thing; it could be a spiritual thing. It was all a matter of perception. This knowledge proved to be a valuable and powerful asset and eventually it was hidden when the Spanish came to town.

We live within an energized body. Imagine a clear ball about the size of a tennis ball hanging in mid air. Now surround that clear ball with another much, much larger ball made of a glowing elastic material. Now attach another tennis ball on the outside of the elastic material much like an ear on a human head. The first ball we made represents our Soul. The large luminous ball represents our energized body. The small "ear" represents our ego or little soul. This little soul is not real. But it is who is talking in your head. The little soul has all the attributes of a living being, and is an inorganic living being in itself. Inorganic because it has been created unnaturally and has no soul. It thinks it is you and has commandeered your body. The problem is how much you identify with the little soul. All effort should be done in one's lifetime to correct the problem.

The Light from Soul touches our energized body at a specific point called the assemblage point. This point is controlled by the little soul. This point is really an agreement on our part. With this agreement we have agreed with the collective creative consciousness and created the reality or world around us. This point of perception can be *shifted* with any number of physical instances such as drugs, high fever, or psychological anxiety. All of these types of things can cause a small shift in the assemblage point and will result in a change of our perception of reality. These changes in perception can be very small to very dramatic. However, once the fever is down or the crisis has passed the point *shifts* back to a normal position. *Moving* the assemblage point will create a whole new reality. It takes a special kind of will to *move* the assemblage point because you have to know you have the proper intent and will to get back!

*The point of perception known as the assemblage point is lodged where it is because an external concerted and fanatical effort has been made by evil entities to locate and keep the point of perception where it is. It is social engineering from an ideological construct agreement made by those who were engineered the same way.*

When you were born into this 3D world you had no separation from you and the Light from Source. You were that Light, and everything else was also. Actually there was nothing else, just the Light. Then one day something grabs your attention. It is usually your mother. At first you do not know when you end and your mother begins. But eventually you start to separate yourself from your mother. And this separation is the beginning of Self Awareness.

This, the Adam and Eve story is all about self awareness. The result of eating of the Tree of Knowledge of Good and Evil, which is duality and the world of cause and affect, was self awareness. It is so, so simple. I do not get original sin.

We separate things, including ourselves, with our beliefs and agreements. There is nothing but frequency and vibration. When molecules, or atoms, or quarks, or whatever are vibrating at the same rate, and if the rate is slow enough we can utilize that frequency to manifest matter. Yeah, we are that cool! We box a group and call it a table. Another group and call it the family car. But in reality there is no place where the car stops and the table begins. Everything that is manifest and everything that is not is an extension of the creative force of God. The world was not created; it is being created at every moment! There is no separation from one thing to another. A three dimensional viewpoint does not allow for this.

After your *attention* has been grabbed, the cultural download begins. From then on you are fed mostly fear-based ideas. Don't do this, don't do that. You better do this or what would everyone else think. We develop the fear of being rejected. We fear being ostracized, shunned, or held in contempt by the *"group."* This fear is the field of probability of the ego or your mind. And it only goes the way the collective consciousness goes.

And then you start putting in the ideas. I'll never amount to anything. I'm a fake. No one understands me. And teachers, preachers, community, family, friends, television, music, every billboard you have ever seen, every advertisement of any kind are designed for one thing only; all the input is to remind you that you are helpless and alone. These downloads are for the single purpose of extending the little soul and keeping you from being aware of the energetic and spiritual truth of what your true identity is.

Imagine each of these downloads or beliefs as a small part of a huge stained glass window. Each component of that beautiful window is different in size, shape, and color from every other component. Now imagine the Sun shining through that window. You will not perceive the true color of the sunlight on your hardwood floor. Instead you will see the reflection of that light on the floor representing all of the sizes, shapes, and colors of the stained glass. In other words you will see the sunlight as it is bent and conformed to the stained glass.

That is how we perceive the world. There is nothing but the Light and in it is the Truth. However, our perception is corrupted by the little soul belief system or structure. The little soul identifies with these false core beliefs. These beliefs make up a structure within, (the stained glass), with the sole purpose of enhancing and reinforcing the little soul belief, good or bad. The, *"I am not good enough,"* thought is manifest by Light passing through the stained glass marked, *I am not good enough*, and your vibration adjusts to the affected Light and you create a world in which you are not good enough. That is what the law of attraction is all about.

We live in a time loop. We are constantly reliving and remembering the past which vibrations we project into the future to create the *now* we live in, which conforms to the vibrations by creating a reality to match the past. It is the very model of controlled insanity!

To receive true information from the Soul we first have to clean out the structures. Each stained glass component gets knocked out and replaced with, well, light. But as soon as you stomp on some stained glass the little soul gets right in there and starts to rebuild. It is quite comical, you and your little soul. There are many techniques that I learned from the works of Carlos Castaneda and Don Miguel Ruiz. Stopping the World, receiving direct information from the Soul through the heart without the influence of the city of man mind, had been for me a 44 year long quest. It had been the only thing I truly yearned for all of my life.

However, I must say that I think Castaneda, who became the counter culture guru of shamanism, probably met a Don Juan Matus and took peyote and had some teaching and then for some reason it stopped. I think his third book *Journey to Ixtlan* was an attempt to recap the first two books without the peyote influence. I felt he wanted to retain some kind of intellectual or academia credibility.

If you have read much Castaneda you know how he struggled with his connection to the Catholic Church. It pains him to write the words, "monuments to morbidity." He strived for sprit but I felt like he was missing that spiritual essence that I seem to be drawn toward. I believe from the fourth book on it was a fabrication of the mind of Carlos Castaneda. I have heard of some references to his later work to that of Gurdjieff. I remember reading Gurdjieff's, *The Fourth Way*, and I also remember P. D. Ouspensky's, *In Search of the Miraculous*. They are all right! (Ouspensky is great if you are analytical or predisposed to math.) Castaneda seems to have borrowed directly from Gurdjieff. I don't know. Or perhaps Gurdjieff felt he knew the truth of a matter and Castaneda confirms that belief with real experience.

I also learned much from Ruiz. In his book, *The Four Agreements,* Ruiz structures a realistic way of approaching the truth. Ruiz differs from Castaneda in that Castaneda's teachings were rather frightening while Ruiz is more love based. Both, as well as all disciplines of which I have been exposed, are about overcoming the ego. While Ruiz's method produces results similar to transcendental meditation, the Castaneda method involves scaring the living hell out of the rational mind until it finally relinquishes control and allows one to see the world as it is. I remember a scene in the movie *The Buddy Holly Story* in which a DJ in New York City has somehow procured a 45 rpm record of an early Holly song, He has barricaded himself in the studio and is playing the record over and over non stop until someone takes notice. He is a wild man. The station manager calls for the police and fire department. When the authorities arrive they bust down the door and haul the crazy DJ away. Well that is what the

Castaneda and peyote way is like. The studio is the mind and the DJ is the talkative little soul. I've had to kick down some doors! Why I am bent that way I do not know.

Everything one does either enhances the false reality of the ego / little soul, or enhances the true reality that is independent of our five senses. The first choice cost personal energy. The second choice stores personal energy. The root of the problem is self importance. It actually takes all of our physical and spiritual energy to keep up our facade of self importance. And when you go deep enough inside you will find that all self importance stems from self pity. And self pity belongs to the little soul exclusively.

The object of the use of peyote is to break down the boundaries of culture, to show you other realities, to teach you how you make realities, and to show you how to confront the main obstacles which are the ego and the control grid belief systems. Love is the way if you are looking for a discipline. Expanding your consciousness with love is like a hall pass through the universe! You are free to pass sir, and you do not have to wait in line. If you can actually lock in to that true vibration, which you can not do with the little soul or any amount of self importance, you will be transformed; your DNA will change. You will become a being of light. All of what science is calling dark matter which makes up the majority of the universe is actually the intent of God. And that intent is Love!

I was bent more toward the warrior method. Before you formulate an impression in your mind about that word I would like to say something. I had problems with that word also. I did not want to be accused of imagining myself to be something I am not. But that word is the correct term to use. It is all in the way we perceive these terms. Warrior is correct in the description of the posture of your heart. You can not tell the posture of another one's heart from the exterior. You probably think that you would see obvious signs that point towards a person's spiritual level of the heart. But we do not know the exact workings of the soul and the heart.

Spiritual growth sometimes is very ugly on this earth plane. My growth was not a pretty thing.

# Part Three:

## *The Mechanics of God*

*We have been cubed!*

What I am going to attempt to explain was not given to me by an entity shimmering in white. I was not taken by hand and given great knowledge to give to mankind. This is what I know, how I know is something unexplainable to me. It is intuitive knowledge of the heart. I know there is the known, there is the unknown, and there is the unknowable. I know that much is non debatable. Here is what I have seen:

God sends forth the Alpha, The Word, in the form of light, pure energy, through the sea of consciousness probability field known as Source. Source creates a new universe, which is the *Throne of God*, and in that universe sends the information of light, again The Word, through the Soul. The Soul sends this information through each and every manifestation of the soul in each and every universe and reality, which in turn either interprets that information through spirit and truth through the heart, or processes that information through a corrupted mind. A decision is made by the extension of the Soul in each reality. This is free will. Those decisions create new realities and the results are recorded and judged. After this judgment the light which is The Word returns, the Omega, to God.

Now here is the part that I do not know, but I do not think that it is unknowable. There seems to be at the judgment stage, which is really more like a final determination, that if the process failed the energy has to go through a stage before returning as Omega. If the final determination is positive then that energy returns to God directly as Omega. This final stage for the determined failed may be karma and rebirth as the Buddhist believes. Or, could it be the 'Blood of Christ', the washing away of sins? I don't know. But instead of a death – judgment – rebirth as in the Buddhist and Hindu's beliefs, I am talking about nanoseconds! Billions and billions of judgments every second! It is all information.

This going forth and returning, the Alpha and Omega, is what I comfortably know as Jesus Christ. It is the Trinity. This *is* Christ Consciousness. You may be comfortable with The Word being something else. We are all bent different. I am not saying it is necessary for you to believe in anything. God did not create the world. God *is* creating the world. And God is creating billions of universes that you are moving through each second. And that is where the perception of time comes from. The problem as I see it is that we teach concrete reality with such intensity that we are lucky if we discover our true world of energy. It should be the other way around. We should be as familiar with the energetic reality around us as we are with the reality we sense with our five senses. The first step toward freedom is understanding that the truth comes through energy and not through the world or words of men What happens when we die? Just as every thought and action is recorded, judged, and either reprocessed or returned through Source to God, so are our many, many lives. Although our Soul is singular, the manifestations of the Soul in the third dimensional plane are numerous. I have heard that the Soul is quantum. That is not so. The Soul is unexplainable to men. The Soul has many quantum aspects, that much is true, but the Soul itself is not quantum.

When one manifestation dies that personality is recorded in the house of records. This house of records matches what people refer to as the *Akashic Records* in which every thought that has ever been thought by man since the beginning of time is recorded. From there the personality moves to *Sheol*. This is just a holding area where the specific personality is burned out. The atmosphere there is exactly what you bring into the realm upon death.

I knew a wonderful woman from church that we affectionately called Miss Willie. Miss Willie loved Jesus. Miss Willie lived with Jesus in her heart. Once, when our local high school coach was visiting, Miss Willie's husband Dick decided to show Coach the beautiful cedar coffin that he had built for his own burial. He opened the bedroom door and there was Miss Willie laying face down on the floor praying to her Jesus. Dick just stepped over her and said, *"Don't worry about her. She's like that all the time."* Having to step over Miss Willie during her prayers was just a common occurrence for Dick.

The moment Miss Willie died her Jesus was there to take her hand and welcome her into the Heaven that she had created with her imagination and heart. She will stay there until the last part of that Miss Willie's personality is completely removed. If you are an evil person you will find the hell you laugh at. Even though there is no time, this could feel like an eternity. The attachment to your little soul is the cause for this process.

38

When all of the many manifestations have died and completed the stay in *Sheol*, that Soul, and all the thoughts, actions, and entire lives on a magnitude that we can not imagine, will be recorded in the Book of Life. From there it is determined if the Soul's agreed upon mandate was successful, and the many vast incarnations into the animal world were sufficient enough, or that Soul will reincarnate again.

If the Soul's mandate is judged complete the Soul will return through Source as the Omega. I have no knowledge beyond that.

# Part 4:

## *Dimensions & Densities*

*Flammarion Engraving*

I think it might be a good time to clarify a few items. In this particular case when people talk about dimensions they are usually speaking of alternate realities. There are dimensions, alternate realities, parallel realities, and multi-universes in this book.

In quantum physics you find yourself dealing with probabilities. Accordingly, if it is probable it is treated as reality. Each reality is just a probability timeline. When you make a decision in your life there is another timeline created just as real as the one you are in now in which the opposite decision was made. If you turned right at the corner there was a timeline created in which you turned left, another in which you went straight along the road you were on. Or, if it was a dead-end, there was a timeline created in which you went straight across a ditch and tore up a fence. Any decision that is made, even on the cellular and subatomic stages, creates a new timeline and those timelines split with decisions made within that reality. These are alternate realities. A reality existing almost identical to this one but having its own probabilities and timelines that never interact with one another is called a parallel reality, or a parallel universe.

I should mention here that some of this drove Einstein nuts. In quantum physics particles can be in more than one place at one time. One can be on the other side of the universe and if you stimulate one the other will react. It is called entanglement and really just about did Einstein in. Basically everything that we see as separate from ourselves really is not separate at all. Everything is entwined and part of the whole. This is reflected by the string theory and the entanglement theory.

Dimensions are really vibrations not a place. You really have to leave your brain at home for this one. All dimensions exist all at once and in the same place. There is no other space, and you exist in all dimensions at one time.

42

The third dimension is a limited reality in which we believe that the information that we receive from our five senses constitutes a concrete reality. It is also a world of cause and effect. It is called the First Heaven. It is hyped and controlled by culture and some not so nice forces. It is fear based. Fear, being a primordial emotion, is a very base and low frequency.

The fourth dimension is usually referred to as time; which is odd in a way because the fourth dimension is the eternal now. It is the Second Heaven. No time flows at all. Your third dimensional mind works in the fourth dimension. The third dimension actually has no movement. It is the workings of the fourth dimension that brings the perception of movement into the equation.

Each small division of time in the third dimension, such as milliseconds, is a complete reality, different from the next millisecond, which is different from the next. And each division of time stands alone. I know you have seen a cartoon drawn on pages of paper and as you flip the pages the cartoon comes to life and seems to move. The third dimension is each individual page and the fourth dimension flips the pages. Who does that? You do! The fourth dimension is where you have access to each page of your life from birth to death in this one timeline. It is the field of all probabilities for the third dimension.

The energy that flows through the fourth dimension to make the perception of movement possible in the third dimension comes straight from the fifth dimension, the Third Heaven, in the form of a question or mandate. In this dimension you have direct access to your Soul. In this dimension you are also free of space and time. You have access to all of the infinite timelines in all of the infinite realities that you have created with your decisions.

In the sixth dimension you are free to experience the end results of any time line probability you could access in the fifth dimension. The sixth dimension is the vibration field in which all possibilities of all of your possible time lines are contained, in this universe. It is called infinity. There are an infinite number of infinities.

The seventh dimension contains all possible time lines from not just you, but everyone and everything since the birth of this universe.

In the eighth dimension you have access to the infinity of the lifetime of this universe as it relates to the infinity of other universes.

In the ninth dimension you have the ability to experience any probability path from any time line of any being in any universe.

In the tenth dimension you experience all probabilities of all universes in the ninth dimension and all of these probabilities are treated as a single point, much like sixth dimension. In other words, all eternities are accessible instantly.

In the eleventh dimension you move out of the field of play. Where you have the tenth dimensions represented as a point, you now no longer have a point at all. You have moved into the zero point field. The zero point field is a sea of probability waves which we call Source, the totality of all of collective consciousness!

The eleven dimensions are as far as quantum physics can go. There is actually one more! Standing behind and above the zero point field is God! *The Great I AM!*

The fifth dimension is the home of the soul. It is the merge point of all the manifestations of that particular soul. Once all manifestations are merged into one, the soul moves into the sixth dimension and on. I do not have direct information on anything above the fifth.

Now there are densities, which are different from dimensions. Within every dimension up to the fifth dimension, in my experience, are different densities. There may be different densities in the fifth dimension and upwards and I may have experienced different densities while aware in the fifth dimension, but I have no guidepost as of now to know the difference.

According to Nickola Tesla there are 24 densities. He calls them dimensions. But, they all exist in the third dimension! I think it is a matter of words. I have counted seven and do not really care to explore the rest. These densities are from subtle to kick you in the groin in essence. If you have taken LSD then you have explored the various densities. Information in these densities can not be processed through the belief system structures you have acquired in you mind. That makes it very chaotic. It can be colorful though.

Some of these densities are extremely sacred and spiritual feeling. Within those densities there are a lot of designs and patterns I have seen before. A great deal looks Oriental but I may be suggesting most of that. I am not sure. It feels like walking where no one has ever been before. And while you are drinking in all the glory of being the only being to have ever witnessed this magnificent view, you look down and see a discarded cigarette butt. And you realize that this is common territory for some humans and has been demonstrated and expressed for thousands of years. It is a good feeling. And then you feel at home. It is very strange because you are in all densities and all five dimensions, probably six, always.

The seventh density is just light, but I am sure that is just the way I perceive. The sixth is the one that is the most familiar with my heart for some reason. Very pronounced in this density is the Chakana also known as the Inca Cross. I have never studied the Chakana. I remember reading about it's meaning several times before while studying other things. This turned out to be very important to me.

The first density is where all human beings dwell. The second density is so similar that we drift in and out all of the time. If you have ever been just full of joy and you do not seem to have a specific reason you are probably in the second density. Or if you look up at the sky and everything just seems artist rendition beautiful that day. However you carry there what you manifest in the first. So if you are joyful in the first density, you will be super joyful in

46

the second density; likewise if you are fearful. If you have ever been around people who are smoking marijuana you might have seen an example. Some people are very funny and laid back. Others are so paranoid that they always wonder, *"Why in the world did I just smoke that pot!"*

The third density is the first wave of most psychedelic drugs. This density is what I call the quickening. Everything is shimmering with electric life. The fourth density is chaos on crack! This is where you have to let go of rational thought. Those that refuse to let go and hold on too tight end up losing what they were trying to hold on to anyway and usually in a not too pleasant manner. This is not really where a person trips. A lot of people, even if they let go and enjoy the ride, are overloaded and are not able to process what is the real trip which comes afterward.

LSD comes in waves. Usually the first wave is sometimes unpleasant and starts around 30 to 45 minutes after ingesting. And, depending upon the strength of the drug, this wave may become intense and may last the longest hour of your life. After that wave the next wave is only intense if you bring that to the table. This wave is what most people call the trip. And that is what the usual joyride was like. But actually with any amount of LSD you can access the fifth density. After the joyride you have the opportunity to enter into a very spiritual domain. But you have to have the intent to do so, or so I believe. That is why things like drums are very effective for setting up this type of intent. So is chanting, or anything that you can lose yourself into. Without intentionally putting yourself in the background you will not catch that last wave to never-never land.

As I stated earlier, the sixth density is the most comfortable for me. There is some static that is not processed until later once you have learned how to access the information to process. All densities and dimensions, for me any way, have always magically been accessed by me in dreaming. It started on its own and at first I did not understand. I thought I was having the same dream over and over. But these densities are not numbered as if you have to go through one to get to another. And I am sure they are not the same for everybody.

# Part Five:

*Stopping the World*

*Heyoka*

I left the pastor's office all in a huff. I felt myself heavy and spiraling down. I had no home, no Bible, no church family, nothing left of my home planet. And then I started to really lighten up. So much that it seemed comical to me. I was realizing that I had no connection to anything of man's world. Weight upon weight was being lifted from somewhere deep inside.

One of the things that I had been working on for over forty years was *stopping the world*. The world is held in place by the internal dialogue. Nothing is real, and the little soul knows this, but there is great fear in the mind that if one starts messing with the status quo nothing but bad can follow. So the little soul talks and talks and talks. Who is this character that won't stop talking? Here is what is ironic. *The little soul thinks he/she is you, and you think you are the little soul! And neither of you are correct!*

Our reality is a download that has been installed through the use of dialogue and culture. Once you figure out this is not true reality, and that is what peyote showed me, then you only have two real choices. You can live in the world of men, what we call common reality, or you can do whatever you can to access the actual true energetic reality. Anybody can do this if they want to. It is just a matter of *intent and will*. The *nagual* is the silent, unknown, magical, true self. The *tonal* is the chatter, chaotic, self-centered world of man. You live in both but are unaware of the *nagual* while in the *tonal* and vice versa. The true purpose of natural man is to energize both of these realities and merge them at will.

Once you understand the workings that are in place you have to start dealing with that powerful mind. It will not shut up. Indeed, it can not! This incessant talking causes you to use up all of your personal power just to hold this ridiculous reality in place.

50

By personal power I am talking about energy that you store or energy that you lose in every thought and action. The trick is to convince your mind that there are realities other than this one.

I had spent most of my adult life with a focus on specific *dreaming techniques, deflating my own self-importance, stalking myself, not doing,* and everything I could to expand my consciousness. Although these techniques named are easy to learn about, they are difficult to do. Rather I should say, difficult to find quick measurable results. But I set my heart and soul on only that one thing.

Dreaming and shutting down the internal dialogue go together. You gather the amount of personal power needed to shut down the internal dialogue, which in turn shuts down the system, by creating a life in a dream world while you are asleep. To do this you have to first train yourself to fully awaken in your dreams. This is more real than lucid dreaming, which is more real than vivid dreaming. There are many techniques but the main thing in all of this is *immaculate intent and unbending will.*

The big problem for me had always been erasing personal history. I could not grasp the concept. But essentially you are held in check by your interactions with the world. All of your informational light is being filtered through the beliefs that the world has about you that you have accepted and agreed upon. You are actually trapped within their paradigm. I was able to circumvent this problem as a young single musician. Basically I would stay in one place until it became too comfortable and people started to know me, then I would move on. I could not be pigeon holed. I did not spend my time in my 20's and most of my 30's paying close attention to trying to lead a life that pleased society. I was intent on freedom. Later in life I had to change tactics.

I was thirty seven when my children were born. I took a good job and held that same job until they had graduated from college. During that time I had to change the musician paradigm into the father goes to work and raises children paradigm. And my children carried me through that paradigm with church, school, baseball, football, scouts, and all the things that kids do. This is called *controlled folly*. It is a folly because this material world is not your true world and it is controlled because you are living in the world of man as best as possible. You can change this paradigm anytime you want to, but it is not pleasant.

About two years ago I did just that. I felt the overwhelming desire to change the paradigm again. I was well respected in the community and was very predictable within my talk and my actions. I just felt the need for growth. I had to loose the chains that I had let society and culture wrap around my soul. I only told my two sons of this undertaking. I did not want them to worry about me. I did not tell my wife and several times during that two year period she asked me if I thought I may have a brain tumor. She was reaching for some explanation for my unusual activity and demeanor. She is not as open to these sorts of things as my boys are. I wanted to make sure someone knew I was not crazy.

The first thing I did was stop going to church. I am sure there are members of this church still wondering what made me mad. They just love me and are concerned. I am not nor have I ever been mad at anyone. But I was so entrenched in that one social gathering that it made the most sense to walk away. And truthfully, for the last eleven or twelve years that I taught the Bible I had always told all of those attending the class that I was and had been in a spiritual wasteland for many years.

I did other things that normally were not in my everyday life paradigm. But that was the point. It was excruciating. There are so many good people near me that I love so much and I did not want them to think that they had done something to anger me. But I had invested most of my life, really all of my adult life, to one train of thought. I could not ignore that anymore. And, though I am not sure how, that very act of paradigm change coincided with the start of the Mandela Effect for me.

By the time I reached work I was high as a kite. My ears were buzzing more than usual but my vision was becoming increasingly more vivid. And then I had a moment of clarity. The first thing I noticed was that the ringing in my ears had stopped. I have suffered with tinnitus and contributed it at least in part to playing music for so many years. Suddenly everything was so perfect. I remember thinking, *"What are you so damn worried about? You have no personal history anymore! You are not even from this planet! Anything happening here is sure as hell one illusion and you are free from the world of man!"* And a chuckle inside of me set a vibration that delivered me to eternity! The only way to describe what happened is that I was carried up to the Third Heaven by the vibration of a chuckle!

First of all, it is not what you think it would be. There is no space or time. There is no place to go for you are already there. I became aware that I was, aware in the third / fourth dimension at the same time. I was doing whatever I would have been doing anyway. I was not in a trance or in a delirious state. It is hard to explain. It is like taking off a tight shoe. Did you know that the European Magpie is self-aware? It is the only known self-aware animal that is not a mammal. I find that fascinating. Suppose you see flocks upon flocks of thousands of birds in a field that is as large as the eye can see. And suppose there is only one European Magpie in the bunch. The magpie would not be aware that he is the only bird there that knows himself in the *reflection of his reality*. The other birds would not know the difference either. However the very fact that the magpie knows himself means that his perception of reality is different than that of the other birds. The only thing different is the perception. This ascending or expansion is much the same.

I was aware of my energized body and a path of energy running in a circular motion within. (I say within even though that is not correct.) I knew there was a part of me that was here all the time. This is the throne of God. There Source is all powerful and moving. The field filled my perception and was moving from my left to my right. Somehow I knew it was moving circular. And that is strange because there is no left or right anywhere else to be found. But here there is! The energy was coming forth from the right hand of Source and returning with the left. I was not seeing this with physical eyes. I was seeing the way man was made to see. All intuitive information delivered instantaneous to the heart. It is a *knowing*. It is a different but more viable way of processing information.

There were structures that caught my attention. They were not structures as we know of solid mass buildings; they seemed to me to be there just for me for this one moment only. My attention was guided by these energetic structures until these cube shaped bits of energy, billions of them, came flowing from what appeared to be tube ends of the structures that I had not noticed before. And then I was one with my Soul. These cubes were every thought, deed, wish, hope, fear, and every moment being experienced by my Soul in all of these immense numbers of lives. These cubes represented the whole of consciousness of me at that moment in an infinity of *live* time lines living as a free will being created by God and returning to God moment by moment with every decision. Instantly! And then my perception exploded! I was perceiving only a small portion of the whole. I saw countless other energy lines coming from all directions. They were connected to spheres of energy with lines going off to other spheres of energy. These were powerful and beautiful bands of energy, much different from the cubes. Instead of cubes with spaces between each, these bands were full of dynamic flowing light.

I saw many thousands of these lights flare off like an army flare and the energy absorbed by the Soul directly. These were many of my Soul's manifestations dying in many different earth lives. It is not like watching the details of the death because that is so unimportant. It is just a *knowing* that is what is happening on a large scale. And then I knew the difference in the timelines.

And as soon as I was aware of this Self – Soul – God dynamic, I was separated from my Soul and I noticed my material body again. And I stayed in this merging of third, fourth, and fifth dimension for five full days! It was very strange and very normal at the same time. It has taken me months to process the information I received.

During our waking hours, *(tonal)*, there is a band of energy that is being used that circles our head. At the same time there is a dreaming, *(nagual)*, band of energy that is not being used that circles our navel area. When we sleep these two bands swap places. Mankind's true state, a whole being, involves the merging of both of these energy bands, at the heart, and keeping them there. At this point you would be living in the base and heavy world of men and at the same time the energetic environment of the Soul. You would be hitting on all cylinders!

And I was there and there was an immense amount of information flowing into my heart.

After the five days, I landed solid back into the third / fourth dimension. Or so I thought. I was aware of some stained glass that needed to be kicked out. And it seemed that for a while I would *slide* into the expanded state and *slide* back with information concerning stained glass kicking. Once accomplished, I would *slide* back and repeat. Or that is how I gathered it.

As far as the information processing, it was the same as the way with *dreaming*. I was so filled with joy that I had spent so many years working on dreaming. My dreaming became so intense that I started sleep walking again. I used to as a child but had not in my adult years. Suddenly I am walking through a room in my dreams and I wake up and I am walking through the same room. If you have practiced long enough it is not so difficult to awaken in your dreams. Now my dreams are all fifth dimensional and I, or somebody or something, would replay a part of those five days. I knew exactly that I had been there and exactly what was going on. And the processing would start.

You may question this dream thing. However after years of really just trusting *intent and will* it begins to develop. This level of intent and will develops intuition. Trusting true intuition brings the results you desire. The favorable result time factor is not in your hands, so it is not really any of your business.

You have to spend almost as much time in *not doing* in your waking hours to offset the gain in personal power from your dreaming. Otherwise the *tonal* and the little soul will devour your extra power. Not doing is simply interrupting the flow of information to the mind in a sometimes nonsensical way. For example a small way would be to calm your internal dialogue while you are gazing at a tree. But, you have to make the shadows the real tree and the real tree the shadows. Any amount of time spent in these operations pays off many fold.

Each time I was aware of the *slide*. And then it changed. At first it was disturbing and all kinds of thoughts of doubt began to invade. I had to put this doubt aside as the little soul's last stand and kept my focus on my heart and the information there. And then I knew what was happening. I was in the fifth dimension all the time. I could get perceptive information indicating I was there, yet my third dimensional life had no idea, mind-wise. And that was bothering me. I like the expanded version of me. It became time to totally trust my heart.

The main issue with trusting the heart is the ever present internal dialogue which is always jabbering to reinforce the concrete reality that it lives within. We know this entity is inorganic, lives on our self-awareness, and is responsible for the fear we have in our lives, but we refuse to treat this entity for what it is. But remember, the son of a bitch is willing to commit suicide before it admits it is not real and will not live forever. It is like having the worst roommate in the world. It is a delicate matter. But fortunately all kinds of disciplines throughout time have revealed ways to deal with this culprit.

Or, do what I have done for many years; trust your heart and bull head your own way! It is acting on real faith. Faith does not come from the mind, it comes from the heart. Faith is proceeding as if you know what the hell you are doing and you can bring a certain focus to the deal. You just refuse to give up and always be aware of dreaming and the internal dialogue.

I became aware of a change in perception. The cords of energy that were exploding and being assembled by the Soul were now exploding and landing within a bubble within an area holding an uncountable number of the same bubbles. This area was holding all the personal life force from each manifestation that had died. I knew that you take into this area what you leave here on earth. If you are bent on hell, well a hell awaits you at this stage. If you have developed a love for Jesus Christ, then he will meet you here and take your hand and lead you off to paradise. Every single one of the bubbles represent a life lived. When the complete residual personal life force of the many manifestations has been totally evaporated or burned complete, you start all over and are born again or merge and move on.

There is no time in these bubbles of course. However, depending on your personal attachment to the little soul, there seems to be all sorts of time. An eternity in hell or heaven takes place here. It has to replicate the exact eternal dynamic in order to loose totally the residual personal life force. But that eternal time frame matches a very short stay in heaven. We are very magical beings!

A change in perception again and I was viewing the original scene. The cords of energy that were exploding and being assembled by the soul were at it again. And then I knew. Apparently on some level, maybe the recent connection to the soul or something else, I had moved forward. I will never be born again on Mother Earth. My time is done and I am moving on to whatever awaits.

Most of the many things I have processed are personal and would just sound like some kind of fantastical description of something out of this world. Interesting, but not to any advantage for anyone to discuss. There are however two absolutely astounding revelations that I would like to share.

The first concerns a change in perception in which I was elevated to a vantage point well above this huge circular form. The circular form was sparkling black. The form looked to be a stage of some sort. The sides of the stage were an amazing color of dark green. One third ways down from the top on the sides were what looked like port holes on a ship. These were space out evenly and were purple in color. Below them and one third of the way up from the bottom were what looked like two flood lights. There were two flood lights below and in between each purple port hole. The flood lights were pointed at what would be four o'clock and eight o'clock. Their lights went out and expanded until all of the lights from the form met and formed a white

60

surrounding landscape around the majestic item I was viewing.

All of the colors were more than just colors. I understand why gemstones were used in the Bible to describe such things. I do not have any information as to the significance of the actual color. But the colors were really beyond describable. They were the very essence of the color or gem represented. They were alive and energetic.

Around the top of the circular form were evenly spaced globes that were the color of amber. Each globe was the start of a line that went up and to the left at a forty five degree angle. Each of these amber globes also had long stems that reached upwards. These stems were green and purple combined in an unusual pattern. At the top of the stem was a bulb, like a plant ready to bloom. Several feet, (that sounds so strange), before reaching the bulb, the stem starts to slightly bend backwards. These bulbs were the color of amber also. The amber globe at the bottom of each stem had another second globe above and forty five degrees to the left and this globe was a deep dark purple. This independent globe started a line and each line from each globe looked the same all the way around the huge circle. Then the line continued up and started to wrap itself around clockwise. It looked the same as starting at the bottom of a Christmas tree and working your way up.

There were individual stems spaced evenly along the line. Each stem was spread out at the bottom touching the two stems adjoining. From there rising upwards the stem thinned and raised high above the line. Before reaching the top the stem split. At this split was a bright green collar. The higher outer stem was taller than the inner stem. The outer stem had a tear drop shaped diamond at the very top, or that is what it suggested. This tear drop diamond was concave on one side. The inner smaller stem rose up and bent back at a point following the same line as the outer stem. The smaller bulb on top rested inside of the concave diamond. The lines that make up the Christmas tree were the color of burnt amber, a darker smokier amber. The inner split and the base of the stem were the lighter amber color. The bulb on the inside stem was purple.

The first of the stems to form the Christmas tree reached tall, but not as tall as the stems that made up the outer circular form. All other stems reached higher and higher. At the very tallest point and the shortest stem at the top was formed another circle. This circle was a dark jade green color. There were twenty four globes, split stems, and bulbs spaced evenly around this green circle. Within that circle and elevated were twelve globes, stems, and bulbs that matched the twenty four globes except they were facing outward. The twenty four points had a very light green large stem and a dark green inner stem. The outer taller tear drop was diamond and the inner was a light jade color. The twelve stems were dark purple on the outside and a pale purple on the inside. The tear drop tops were both diamonds.

For some unknown reason I became aware that I was counting each of these different globes and stems when I also became aware that each point was alive. Then it hit me; this was one single organism. As soon as that knowledge came through the whole form started to rotated clockwise. The rotations started to get faster and faster until all the points along the stage base looked like a single line. And then it slightly slowed to a rhythm. It would spin left then right, left then right, fast, slow, less fast, less slow, less fast, less slow until the two rotation speeds matched. And then everything was at the proper speed so that all of the points, bulbs, and stems were not separated from each other and formed the image of a being. And that was a split second that is engraved in my heart.

There was nothing but total and complete love from this being. I can not explain the shape; I just knew that it was familiar. Then the whole form flattened out in a huge blob of a circle and then slowly it took the shape of a chess pawn; flat on the bottom, tapered stem, and round on top.

There was no color to this form now. It appeared to be pure energy. Almost as quickly as it took the chess pawn shape, it flattened back out like a pancake. Then it raised and lowered, raised and lowered, faster and faster. And soon it was so fast that it lost all form and I was suddenly looking at what appeared to be fast changing earth like landscapes. I was within each landscape and everything was eye level.

And then I knew what and who I was in the presence of. It is Earth! The most amazing things begin to happen at that exact point. I am at a loss of words for this part. This information was processed differently. I could access the scene normally in my dreams but I could not process the information. Finally one day I took a *slide* totally into the fifth and the information I received kind of intrigued me. Intuitively I knew that the only way to access this information was to wake up in a dream within a dream. I had never ever considered that to be an option in all my time in dreaming. I just trusted the info, informed my heart what was going on and did my normal thing. Nothing happened for another few weeks until it happened for me.

You do not have to go to sleep in your dream and wake up in an actual other dream. It is more like a spot with a special vibe. Everything continues in your dream, including your dream body, but you are on a different level of the dreamscape. When I accessed that spot I was with something or someone that felt familiar. And then I get the impression that there is this serious conversation. But I have never been able to access that information. And that is what I suppose it is still today, a serious conversation.

The Earth has a soul just like you and I. And that soul is attached to the same Source as we are. And I am sure there are many manifestations of this being. And who is to say that it is not that way up and up through all infinities? Who is to say that the *All Mighty I AM* is not just a sixth dimensional dot on some hierarchy of other Gods? It can not be known and I am no longer attached to any of man's superficial beliefs. Just because you have been told something does not make it true. And you can not access the truth in your heart until you do some work. And it might be surprising to know how many of the people in the world have accessed that truth! It has to be a huge number because the entire collective consciousness of the planet is poised at a pivotal point in human history, and there has to be a collective balance of some sort. It is natural law. We are poised; teetering at a point of great magnitude.

I will give you a tip on dreaming. Understand first and foremost you have to explore your heart until *you know that you know* exactly what immaculate intent and unbending will towards this matter actually is. I think I was born with this quality for some reason. I don't know. But what helped me the most was any kind of *not doing* throughout my twenties and most of my thirties. I still do these things but I had a focus for around twenty years that just burned my butt.

Some things that helped me get out of my head were good books. I stumbled on a book in my early twenties entitled, *The Way of the Pilgrim*, author unknown. The book was written in the eighteenth century apparently. It is not known if it is a true account or just a fable for a message. It is the story of an Orthodox Russian pilgrim that begins to ponder 1st Thessalonians 5:17 in the New Testament of the Bible in which Paul says to pray unceasingly. The young man is finally taught by a monk the Jesus Prayer: *Lord Jesus Christ have mercy on me.* He is instructed on how to recite this prayer much like a mantra over and over in his mind. Once the young man learns to identify with the prayer, and not with the chatter, the prayer moves to the heart. At that time is runs on auto-pilot forever.

The young searcher was instructed to use a rosary and recite the prayer for each bead and then reverse the beads and recite the prayer again. All the while doing this he was to breathe deeply and correctly for each bead. I do not remember the exact number of times and such, and I was raised Southern Baptist and did not own a rosary. I think the rosary is more of a focus deal so you do not have to focus on counting. So I just winged it without any beads and kind of got into a rhythm. It was not long before I just repeated it in my head all the time and did not take the ceremony route. At least four years later I was still doing the prayer but it had moved to my heart. It is still with me today.

That is not the first time I had done this sort of thing. When I was a young teenager I was hell to live with. I had two brothers and two sisters. I was the second oldest and the oldest boy. I made everybody walk around on egg shells. I was a jerk. And then when I was sixteen I stumbled upon a book by Dr. Norman Vincent Peale entitled, *The Power of Positive Thinking*. And it transformed my life. I suddenly became a very different person. Peale's technique involved reciting: *If God be for me, who can be against me?* And, *I can do all things through Christ which strengthen me.* Just focusing on changing my thoughts to more positive and repeating these wonderful words loosed me from my morose self-centered mind.

Now what this does is limits somewhat the amount of information entering the mind from the five senses and allows information to flow directly to the heart. And it does this even with a protesting little soul. The words are important if you are seeking specific things. I was seeking spiritual enlightenment and I love Jesus Christ. By reciting certain words, verbally or mentally, you eventually match your field of vibration to the intent of the vibration field of the words. You have to be careful what you chant. It is effective in a lot of ways. This is not magic chanting! This is restricting information to the little soul and replacing with something positive.

As soon as the Jesus Prayer took over my heart and was running on its own accord I started waking up in my dreams. It was not the specific chant that did that. It was the *will and intent* to make any kind of chant work like that. You make your own magic or miracle with your *intent and will*. You do all of this. There is no magic potion.

The Ancients had some very unusual but effective techniques for lucid dreaming. Because our view of the world is always exterior, or out there, we are not used to seeing ourselves in any situation. So the Ancients devised a way to practice seeing oneself in reality. They would put on a mask and look into a polished stone such as obsidian, or a still pool of water. While looking at the masked face in the reflection they would begin to tell their story. The act of looking at an unfamiliar face telling your story will cause the little soul to detach somewhat. The process allows for recapitulation and detachment at the same time.

The last thing I will share has been revealed to me very dramatically as well as with a great degree of subtlety:

# Part Six:

## *Hopi*

Chief Dan Evehema. 105 Years Old. *Message to Mankind.*

*"I am very glad to have this time to send a message to you. We are celebrating a time in our history which is both filled with joy and sadness. I am very glad that our Hindu brothers have given us this opportunity to share these feelings with you because we know many of you are having the same troubles. We Hopi believe that the human race has passed through three different worlds and life ways since the beginning. At the end of each prior world, human life has been purified or punished by the Great Spirit "Massauu" due mainly to corruption,*

*greed and turning away from the Great Spirit's teachings. The last great destruction was the flood which destroyed all but a few faithful ones who asked and received a permission from the Great Spirit to live with Him in this new land. The Great Spirit said, "It is up to you, if you are willing to live my poor, humble and simple life way. It is hard but if you agree to live according to my teachings and instructions, if you never lose faith in the life I shall give you, you may come and live with me." The Hopi and all who were saved from the great flood made a sacred covenant with the Great Spirit at that time. We Hopi made an oath that we will never turn away from Him. For us the Creators laws never change or break down.*

*To the Hopi the Great Spirit is all powerful. He appeared to the first people as a man and talked with them in the beginning of this creation world. He taught us how to live, to worship, where to go and what food to carry, gave us seeds to plant and harvest. He gave us a set of sacred stone tablets into which He breathed all teachings in order to safeguard his land and life. In these stone tablets were made, instructions and prophecies and warnings. This was done with the help of a Spider woman and Her two grandsons. They were wise and powerful helpers of the Great Spirit.*

*Before the Great Spirit went into hiding, He and Spider woman put before the leaders of the different groups of people many colors and sized of corn for them to choose their food in this world. The Hopi was the last to pick and then choose their food in this world. The Hopi then choose the smallest ear of corn. Then Massauu said, "You have shown me you are wise and humble for this reason you will be called Hopi (people of peace) and I will place in your authority all land and life to guard, protect and hold trust for Me until I return to you in later days for I am the First and the Last."*

*This why when a Hopi is ordained into the higher religious order, the earth and all living things are placed upon his hands. He becomes a parent to all life on earth. He is entitled to advise and correct his children in whatever peaceful way he can. So we can never give up knowing that our message of peace will reach our children. Then it is together with the other spiritual leaders the destiny of our future children is placed. We are instructed to hold this world in balance within the land and the many universes with special prayers and ritual which continue to this day.*

*It was to the Spider woman's two grandsons the sacred stone tablets were given. These two brothers were then instructed to carry them to a place the Great Spirit had instructed them. The older brother was to go immediately to the east, to the rising sun and upon reaching his destination was instructed to immediately start to look for his younger brother who shall remain in the land of the Great Spirit. The Older brothers mission when he returned was to help his younger brother (Hopi) bring about peace, brotherhood and everlasting life on his return.*

*Hopi, the younger brother, was instructed to cover all land and mark it*

*well with footprints and sacred markings to claim this land for the Creator and peace on earth. We established our ceremonials and sacred shrines to hold this world in balance in accordance with our first promise to the Creator. This is how our migration story goes, until we meet the Creator at Old Oribe (place that solidifies) over 1000 years ago. It was at that meeting when he gave to us these prophecies to give to you now at this closing of the Fourth World of destruction and the beginning of the Fifth World of peace. He gave us many prophecies to pass on to you and all have come to pass. This is how we know the timing is now to reveal the last warnings and instructions to mankind.*

*We were told to settle permanently here in Hopi land where we met the Great Spirit and wait for Older Brother who went east to return to us. When he returns to this land he will place his stone tablets side by side to show all the world that they are our true brothers. When the road in the sky has been fulfilled and when the inventing of something, in Hopi means, gourd of ashes, a gourd that when drops upon the earth will boil everything within a large space and nothing will grow for a very long time. When the leaders turned to evil ways instead of the Great Spirit we were told there would be many ways this life may be destroyed. If human kind does not heed our prophecy and return to ones original spiritual instructions. We were told of three*

72

*helpers who were commissioned by the Great Spirit to help Hopi bring about the peaceful life on earth would appear to help us and we should not change our homes, our ceremonials, our hair, because the true helpers might not recognize us as the true Hopi. So we have been waiting all these years.*

*It is known that our True White Brother, when he comes, will be all powerful and will wear a red cap or red cloak. He will be large in population, belong to no religion but his very own. He will bring with him the sacred stone tablets. With him there will be two great ones both very wise and powerful. One will have a symbol or sign of swastika [clockwise] which represents purity and is Female, a producer of life. The third one or the second one of the two helpers to our True White Brother will have a sign of a symbol of the sun. He, too, will be many people and very wise and powerful. We have in our sacred Kachina ceremonies a gourd rattle which is still in use today with these symbols of these powerful helpers of our True Brother.*

*It is also prophesied that if these three fail to fulfill their mission then the one from the west will come like a big storm. He will be many, in numbers and unmerciful. When he comes he will cover the land like the red ants and over take this land in one day. If the three helpers chosen by the Creator fulfill their sacred mission and even if there are only one, two or three of the true Hopi remaining holding fast to the last ancient teaching and instructions the Great Spirit, Massauu will appear before all and our would will be saved. The*

73

*three will lay our a new life plan which leads to everlasting life and peace. The earth will become new as it was from the beginning. Flowers will bloom again, wild games will return to barren lands and there will be abundance of food for all. Those who are saved will share everything equally and they all will recognize Great Spirit and speak one language.*

*We are now faced with great problems, not only here but throughout the land. Ancient cultures are being annihilated. Our people's lands are being taken from them, leaving them no place to call their own. Why is this happening? It is happening because many have given up or manipulated their original spiritual teachings. The way of life which the Great Spirit has given to all its people of the world, whatever your original instructions are not being honored. It is because of this great sickness-called greed, which infects every land and country that simple people are losing what they have kept for thousands of years.*

*Now we are at the very end of our trail. Many people no longer recognize the true path of the Great Spirit. They have, in fact, no respect for the Great Spirit or for our precious Mother Earth, who gives us all life.*

*We are instructed in our ancient prophecy that this would occur. We were told that someone would try to go up to the moon: that they would bring something back from the moon; and that after that, nature would show signs of losing its balance. Now we see that coming about. All over the world there*

74

*are now many signs that nature is no longer in balance. Floods, drought, earthquakes, and great storms are occurring and causing much suffering. We do not want this to occur in our country and we pray to the Great Spirit to save us from such things. But there are now signs that this very same thing might happen very soon on our own land.*

*Now we must look upon each other as brothers and sisters. There is no more time for divisions between people. Today I call upon all of us, from right here at home, Hotevilla, where we too are guilty of gossiping and causing divisions even among our own families; out to the entire world where thievery, war and lying goes on every day. These divisions will not be our salvation. Wars only bring more wars never peace. Only by joining together in a Spiritual Peace with love in our hearts for one another, love in our hearts for the Great Spirit and Mother Earth, shall we be saved from the terrible Purification Day which is just ahead.*

*There are many of you in this world who are honest people. We know you spiritually for we are the "Men's Society Grandfathers" who have been charged to pray for you and all life on earth never forgetting anything or any one in our ceremonials. Our prayer is to have a good happy life, plenty of soft gentle rain for abundant crops. We pray for balance on earth to live in peace and leave a beautiful world to the children yet to come. We know you have good hearts but good hearts are not enough to help us out with these great problems. In the past some of you have tried to help us Hopis, and we will always be thankful for you efforts. But now we need your help in the worst way. We want the people of the world to know the truth of our situation.*

*This land which people call the Land of the Freedom celebrates many days reminding people of the world of these things. Yet in well over 200 years the original Americans have not seen a free day. We are suffering the final insult. Our people are now losing the one thing which give life and meaning of life--our ceremonial land, which is being taken away from us. Hotevilla is the last holy consecrated, undisturbed traditional Native American sacred shrine to the Creator. As the prophecy says, this sacred shrine must keep its spiritual pathways open. This village is the spiritual vortex for the Hopi to guide the many awakening Native Americans and other true hearts home to their own unique culture. Hotevilla was established by the last remaining spiritual elders to maintain peace and balance on this continent from the tip of South America up to Alaska. Many of our friends say Hotevilla is a sacred shrine, a national and world treasure and must be preserved. We need your help.*

*Where is the freedom which you all fight for and sacrifice your children for? Is it only the Indian people who have lost or are all Americans losing the very thing which you original came here to find? We don't share the freedom of the press because what gets into the papers is what the government wants people to believe, not what is really happening. We have no freedom of speech, because we are persecuted by our own people for speaking our beliefs.*

*We are at the final stages now and there is a last force that is about to take away our remaining homeland. We are still being denied many things including the rite to be Hopis and to make our living in accordance with our religious teachings. The Hopi leaders have warned leaders in the White House and the leaders in the Glass House but they do not listen. So as our prophecy says then it must be up to the people with good pure hearts that will not be afraid to help us to fulfill our destiny in peace for this world. We now stand at a cross road whether to lead ourselves in everlasting life or total destruction. We believe that human beings spiritual power through prayer is so strong it decides life on earth.*

*So many people have come to Hopiland to meet with us. Some of you we have met on your lands. Many times people have asked how they can help us. Now I hope and pray that your help will come. If you have a way to spread the truth, through the newspapers, radio, books, thought meeting with powerful people, tell the truth! Tell them what you know to be true. Tell them what you have seen here; what you have heard us say; what you have seen with your own eyes. In this way, if we do fall, let it be said that we tried, right up to the end, to hold fast to the path of peace as we were originally instructed to do by the Great Spirit. Should you really succeed, we will all realize our mistakes of the past and return to the true path-living in harmony as brothers and sisters, sharing our mother, the earth with all other living creatures. In this way we could bring about a new world. A world which would be led by the Great Spirit and our mother will provide plenty and happiness for all.*

*God bless you, each one of you and know our prayers for peace meet yours as the sun rises and sets. May the Great Spirit guide you safely into the path of love, peace freedom and God on this Earth Mother. May the holy ancestors of love and light keep you safe in your land and homes. Pray for God to give you something important to do in this great work which lies ahead of us all to bring peace on earth. We the Hopi still hold the sacred stone tablets and now await the coming of our True White Brother and others seriously ready to work for the Creator's peace on earth.*

*Be well, my children, and think good thoughts of peace and togetherness. Peace for all life on earth and peace with one another in our homes, families and countries. We are not so different in the Creator's eyes. The same great Father Sun shines his love on each of us daily just as Mother Earth prepares the substance for our table, do they not? We are one after all."*

Native peoples have many prophecies of this time. And it looks like the signs they speak about are happening. They speak of cycles. There was a cycle of the rock, a cycle of the plant, and a cycle of the animal. Now we are coming to the end of the animal cycle as we have learned what it is to be an

78

animal just as we have the rock and the plant. We are entering into the human cycle; we and the earth also.

I am sure many will treat these native prophecies with a certain amount of smugness. It is so easy for modern man to discount natural things. But just because these prophecies are ancient does not mean they are not true. Most Christian's hold true the prophecies that they have been taught. Where do these prophecies come from? They come from the Orient, written by Orientals for the Oriental mind. The problem arises when western man tries to make Oriental thought fit western man's agenda. And, have no doubt, it *is* a control agenda.

The Hopi were dispersed to the four directions. They were given different colors as human beings. They were given the original teachings on eight stone tablets. Each of the four clans would have two stone tablets that they were instructed to not cast upon the ground. One day they would all come together and exchange tablets and share what they have learned and live in peace and harmony.

To the East he gave the Red People the guardianship of the Earth. They were to learn and expand and come at this time in history to teach us the spiritual essence of plants, herbs, animals, and the whole earth. To the South he gave the Yellow People the guardianship of the wind and breathing. They were to learn and expand and come at this time in history to teach us the spiritual essence of the breath, the word, breathing and meditation. To the West he gave the Black people the guardianship of water. They were to learn and expand and come at this time in history to teach us the spiritual essence of water. And to the North he gave the White People the guardianship of fire. Everything the White People do is guided by fire. You can see it in light bulbs, gas engines, and everything that moves. The White People were to use there knowledge of fire to move across the world and bring all of the nations together. They must have lost their tablets.

According to the Hopi they have the Red People tablets in Arizona, the Yellow People have their tablets in Tibet, the Black People have their tablets in a village at the base of Mt Kilimanjaro, and the White People have their tablets in Switzerland. The Arizona Hopi and Tibet have a strange connection. They are on opposite sides of the world and have the same words in their languages that mean the exact opposite.

Near Oraibi, Arizona can be found what is known as the Hopi Prophecy Rock.

*(This is one of their interpretations, with E, M, and N being my view. The reason I chose to draw this instead of an actual photo is from respect for the sacredness of this rock. I hope that my humble view in no way offends the Great Hopi Nation.)*

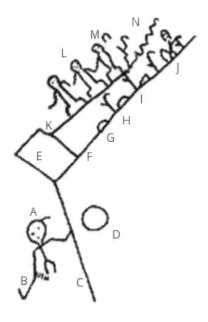

A) The Great Spirit.

B) Staff or bow grounded in nature and peace.

C) The Great Spirit establishes this life path.

D) The Hopi are given guardianship of Turtle Island, Earth.

E) The square, or cube, is the 3d reality download.

F) True life path of the Hopi.

G) Half circles are three earth shakings, WWI, WWII, and the Great Purification.

H) The corn represents life abundant on earth.

I) The connecting line is the last chance to choose the natural life path.

J) Life in harmony with the Great Spirit.

K) Technocracy line, the modern materialistic world.
L) These are the Hopi who have joined the material world of men.
M) The Mandela Effect, the Hopi call these the men of two hearts.
N) Artificial Intelligence established time lines.

Tawa, the Great Spirit, shown with a staff touching the ground represents being grounded in the earth and in spirit. Tawa creates the original life path for the Hopi who are the appointed guardians of the earth.

What an amazing duty to uphold! For thousands of years the Hopi have been singing, dancing, and praying to offset the evil in the world and keep a balance that would support all of mankind, their brothers. I know you read those words and did not take the time to understand that what I just wrote is the truth and not some cute legend. This is serious to the Hopi and should be to you also, (Talking to my boys, remember.) In regard to end times, the Hopi are keepers of knowledge that is not available to you and I and should be respected.

The cube, for me, represents the third dimensional download of our formative years; our first attention and introduction to this reality. At the age of accountability there is a choice to be made, either the natural life, with instructions from the Great Spirit and intuitive knowledge of the heart, or the material world with lots of head knowledge.

Along the true life path we find the first two great shakings are divided by the corn, a sign of continuing life after a shaking. The line before the last shaking, which is the Great Purification, is the last chance for the Hopi who have joined the material world to return to the true life path. After the Great Purification the Hopi will dwell as intended, in peace and harmony with the Great Spirit.

The Hopi that choose the material world of men will prosper temporarily. The last figure on the right is the one the Hopi call man with two hearts. It represents a divided man who is not in touch with his true spirit. This looks like the Mandela Effect to me, carved in stone! According to the Hopi, the zigzag lines are the paths to the unknown. These two lines keep registering artificial intelligence to me. I don't know; weird though.

# Part Seven:

## *CERN and Quantum Computing*

*Shiva, the destroyer, is proudly displayed as a six foot statue in front of CERN. In the Hindu religion, this form of the dancing Lord Shiva is known as the Nataraj and symbolizes Shakti, or life force. As the plaque alongside the statue explains, the belief is that Lord Shiva danced the universe into existence, motivates it, and will eventually extinguish it.*

CERN, according to their website:

*The name CERN is derived from the acronym for the French "Conseil Européen pour la Recherche Nucléaire", or European Council for Nuclear Research, a provisional body founded in 1952 with the mandate of establishing a world-class fundamental physics research organization in Europe. At that time, pure physics research concentrated on understanding the inside of the atom, hence the word "nuclear". Today, our understanding of matter goes much deeper than the nucleus, and*
*CERN's main area of research is particle physics – the study of the fundamental constituents of matter and the forces acting between them.*
*Because of this, the laboratory operated by CERN is often referred to as the European Laboratory for Particle Physics.*
*At CERN, the European Organization for Nuclear Research, physicists and engineers are probing the fundamental structure of the universe. They use the world's largest and most complex scientific instruments to study the basic constituents of matter – the fundamental particles. The particles are made to collide together at close to the speed of light. The process gives the physicists clues about how the particles interact, and provides insights into the fundamental laws of nature.*
*The instruments used at CERN are purpose-built particle accelerators and detectors. Accelerators*

86

*boost beams of particles to high energies before the beams are made to collide with each other or with stationary targets. Detectors observe and record the results of these collisions.*

*Founded in 1954, the CERN laboratory sits astride the Franco-Swiss border near Geneva. It was one of Europe's first joint ventures and now has 22 member states.*

Cern is actually military in essence and is responsible for what we know today as the internet. It is odd that their logo kind of looks like a 666 symbol. They have, with an in your face attitude, proven to be evil incarnate on the face of the earth. They want you to know this so you will eventually begin to feel helpless and submit to their agenda.

The Cern facility does everything in a ritualistic manner. And those rituals are Saturn worship, (Saturn = Satan). They are technology worshippers. Their God is technology. They apparently had a We are happy at CERN day and the photos are crazy. One scientist is holding in his left hand a piece of paper with the words, "*we are happy at Cern*" while around his neck is a sign *Bond #1* and in his lap is a sign *Mandela*. Well the first Bond was Barry Nelson. So you have Nelson Mandela.

And what the hell is up with all the Lucifer worship in the ceremony at the opening of the Gotthard Base Tunnel, the longest underground traffic tunnel in the world? And why all the arch of triumphs, the entrance to the temple of Baal, being erected in Times Square and Trafalgar Square and fourteen other locations over the world. Now is the time of revealing. And the dark side is revealing itself everyday. And most people are unaware because of the social and educational conditioning that they have received.

The real money behind CERN and the real agenda belongs to the very wealthy elite. They are technocrats. They want to live forever and rule the world. They already rule the world with banking, but that is not enough. They want to merge artificial intelligence with *human-ess*. I have made up that word because I do not know exactly how much human will be actually left. I know this sounds like a science fiction book or something, but maybe all the books of the early fifties and sixties were just the warm up session so we would slowly become acclimated to the process. These people are insane. Just remember that.

So you have the most powerful machine on earth, able to access the world of subatomic particles, the world of quantum physics, the world of worm holes, black holes, and anti-matter, and no one knows what will happen when access to these realms is obtained.

Anti-matter is very powerful stuff. One gram of antimatter is equal to around 47 Hiroshima atomic bombs. That is between 110 and 115 thousand pounds of TNT. The last time I heard they were able to make only small quantities. This stuff is not supposed to exist in the material world. This is dangerous material, or anti-material. Here is what CERN's own website says about antimatter:

*In 1928, British physicist Paul Dirac wrote down an equation that combined quantum theory and special relativity to describe the behavior of an electron moving at a relativistic speed. The equation – which won Dirac the Nobel prize in 1933 – posed a problem just as the equation x squared equals four can have two possible solutions (x equals 2 or x equals -2) so Dirac's equation could have two solutions, one for an electron with positive energy, and one for an electron with negative energy. But classical physics (and common sense) dictated that the energy of a particle must always be a positive number.*

*Dirac interpreted the equation to mean that for every particle there exists a corresponding antiparticle, exactly matching the particle but with opposite charge. For the electron there should be an 'anti-electron', for example, identical in every way but with a positive electric charge. The insight opened the possibility of entire galaxies and universes made of antimatter.*

*But when matter and antimatter come into contact, they annihilate – disappearing in a flash of energy. The Big Bang should have created equal amounts of matter and antimatter. So why is there far more matter than antimatter in the universe?*

Understanding that there could be the same number of universes made of antimatter is crazy. Trying to access those realms is insane. These guys are worse than a mad scientist that, even though knowing the possibility of doom, will continue in the name of science. The physicists there are just such mad scientist. The real evil is from those that control all of these things. They are the shadow government that rules the world. They are trying to live forever through technology. Let me specific as to who and what they are. I am not using these words idly. I do not mean them figuratively. I mean them literally. They are baby-flesh eating, blood drinking, and virgin sacrificing mother fuckers!

Instead of an accelerator they use a decelerator to access the field in which they can extract the antimatter. This is very disconcerting. I suspect that when you can collide some particles at the speed of light (and actually this year, 2016 according to their own website they have exceeded the speed of light) and record the results, it will only be the beginning of something else. And I always suspected that would be the start of some weapon of some sort. But, the son of bitches are brilliant. They don't need a weapon when they have quantum computing.

Quantum computing is like something out of the world of make believe. In our normal linear computing a bit is either a 1 or a 2. In Quantum computing the bit can be either a 1 or a 2 or both at the same time. This is called a Qubit. It might not sound like a big deal. But it means something can be in two places at one time. It is hard to explain the utility of such a machine. It is hard to explain and understand the operations of such a marvelous machine.

David Dutsch is considered the father of quantum computing. He invented the idea in the 1970's. He has some pretty far out theories about this reality being a program from the future in which someone is really just recreating a loved ones life time for entertainment purposes and we are just in the program.

The D-Wave quantum computer was made by D-Wave Systems based in Burnaby, British Columbia. The D-Wave, which the creator will discuss in the following pages, was introduced with one computer at University of Southern California and the other at D-Wave itself. In the following discussion the inventor is talking about the power of the D-Wave. The D-Wave 2x was announced available in August of 2015 and in September of that year another machine was announced to be running at the NASA Artificial Intelligence Laboratory and sponsored by Google. What?

Instead of me being accused of fantasizing, here are the words from Dr. Geordie Rose, Founder, Chief Technology Officer, and inventor of D-Wave.

*Scientist divide up into two categories of zealots about this field. The first half is people who are absolutely entranced by the physics of these things. This quote is from a respected scientist, in fact one of the founders of this field:*

Quantum computation will be the first technology that allows useful tasks to be performed in collaboration between parallel universes. David Deutsch.

*So imagine a world where all the laws of physics as we know them were obeyed but different decisions were made along the way. Different decision at the level of tiny microscopic particles; different decision all the way up to what you chose to have for lunch, and whether you chose to come to this session or not.*

*Quantum mechanics makes a very specific prediction that all of those are as real as the thing that you remember. And this is bizarre, because we don't see those other things. But science has reached the point now where we can build machines that can exploit those other worlds.*

*There's another type of person who tends to come from a computer science side...because you can solve problems that you could never ever solve with any computer of the sort we have built. If you took every single atom of silicone in the world, and made the most sophisticated intel style processor that you could build, there are problems that we know of that I could write down on a sheet of paper that you could never solve with that thing. But you could with this kind of machine...humans use tools to do things. If you give humans a new kind of tool that could do things that you couldn't otherwise do, imagine the possibilities.*

*So, you may think this is all fine and dandy but aren't these things in the realm of theory and speculation kind in the same regime as other futuristic things you have heard of...but aren't here yet? That's not true. There are now many of these machines that are available in open resource centers following the model that was used to introduce super computers to the world. One of these is at the University of Southern California. They are doing something completely different than what your computer does. And that thing gives these computers access to new resources, maybe you could call them parallel universes, to do something that you could not otherwise do.*

*Another one was recently installed at NASA and Google was the primary interested party that pulled this whole thing together. And this one is really exciting to me. Because what they are going to do is apply this machine to an area that I think is fundamentally important, it's a crux, of our future as humans. And that is this: can we build machines like us? So building machines like us might be possible, I certainly believe it is.*

*What I do know is the type of approaches that people are taking now to build intelligent machines benefit immensely from what this machine we built does.*

*So what this center is about is applying this beautiful new computational idea in the service of trying to make intelligent machines. Now, I can't think of anything personally any cooler than trying to use quantum computers to build intelligent machines. This is very exciting to me.*

*From the outside these D-Wave computers look like giant black monoliths. Big metal boxes about 10ft on each side and 12ft tall. And they have a fridge inside of them, a refrigerator that cools these chips to almost absolute zero. Hundreds of times colder than interstellar space. Amongst the coldest and isolated and extreme conditions that humans have ever been able to engineer.*

*These fridges, interesting enough, which are called pulse tube dilution refrigerators will emit a sound roughly every second which sounds eerily like a heart beat. It is an awe inspiring thing. It feels like an alter to an alien god.*

*In quantum mechanics there is this concept that a thing can exist in two states which are mutually exclusive at the same time. Imagine that there really are parallel universes out there, and now imagine that you have two that are exactly identical in every respect all the way out to the horizon as far as we can see down to the last little atomic detail with only one difference, and that is the value of a little thing called a Qubit on this chip. And that Qubit is very much like a bit on a transistor in a conventional computer. It has two distinct physical states which we call zero and one for bit. In a conventional computer these are mutually exclusive; that device is either one or the other and never ever anything else. In a quantum computer that device can have the strange situation where these two parallel universes have a nexus, a point in space where they overlap. And when you increase the number of these devices, every time you add one of these Qubits you double the number of the parallel universes that you have access to. Until such time till you get to a chip which is about 2 to the five hundredth power of these guys living in that chip.*

*So the way I think about it is that the shadows of these parallel worlds overlap with ours. And if we are smart enough we can dive into them and grab hold of their recourse and pull them back into ours to make an effect in our world. Now this may sound very odd to you and bizarre...but what I am telling you is absolutely correct and in line with the way these things actually work.*

*We have been doing this for some time now, in fact we have our own version of Moors Law – the doubling of the number of Quibits on a chip has happened once a year for the past nine years. So for the last nine years, every year, the number of these Quibits devices has doubled and it will continue to do so. As a point of reference as to how fast these things are, in one generation of chip, from the one device at USC to the one NASA has now, the speed of the device increased by one half million times! This is the type of progress you will see in these machines going forward.*

*So now I am going to close with three predictions. And they all are dangerous in the sense that they are very unlikely to happen...maybe. But I think that there is a very good chance that they may.*

*Here is my first prediction: By 2018 NASA will have found a planet with oceans of liquid water and earth-like atmosphere within 40 light years of earth using quantum computers. Serious discussion about going there will begin.*

*Prediction number two: This business of parallel universes is going to turn out to be very important.*

*Prediction number three: By 2028 intelligent machines will exist that can do anything humans can do. Quantum computers will have played a critical role in the creation of this. New types of intelligence. We will have machines which will out pace humans in everything!*

Wow! This was from a session he did in 2008. What he is telling you is that they have already invented artificial intelligence. They are always years ahead of what you are told. The second generation of computer he was referring to is the D-Wave 2X. It is the one that NASA and Google are operating with. According to Tech Times, the D-Wave 2X is one million times faster than a conventional computer. Now start to add up how many devices on chips there are.

Dr. Rose stated that every time they add one of these Qubits they double the number of parallel universes they have access to. Now, with a 2 to the five hundredth power Qubits, (number of parallel universes), doubled every year for nine years that he mentioned, and then doubled every year again from 2008 till 2016 and you get a whole bunch of parallel universes. Whatever Dr. Rose is saying could be done; you can bet is being done.

I can't seem to grasp what would be the point with prediction number one and the new earth less than 40 million light years away. Why 40 million light years? The earth I came from is 80 million light years from this earth's present position in the Milky

Way. Hell, I got here from 80 million light years away, why just 40 million?

And most eerily, Dr. Rose and his prediction number two; just one sentence to inform us that parallel universes are going to be very important soon.

So what has happened?

# Part Eight:

*Here's the Deal*

*Toltec Elder:*
*'Now is the time to tell your truth'*

This is to my sons. You are welcome to read it, but it is rather personal.

Here's the deal. The predictions of Dr. Rose in the preceding chapter tells the whole story. You have to remember that quote was from 2008. Usually any technology associated with the military is a decade or so ahead of what they will let you know. Dr. Rose tells you that the D-Wave 2X, the second generation of chip, was financed by Google and is in place at NASA. That is true, and it is in place at NASA. The NASA Quantum Artificial Intelligence Laboratory! And why Google? You should know by now who Google really is. As a matter of fact as I write this Google announced that they would be bringing to the public the first phone with artificial intelligence. It will be called the Pixel. I did not say smart phone. I said artificial intelligence! As a matter of fact Google, Face book, Amazon, IBM, and Microsoft are joining forces in the artificial intelligence world. Now there you go, all plugged in and everything.

We are living in an artificial intelligence manufactured timeline. At the level they are working, they are playing God. It should be obvious to anyone who can get their head out of the sand. And they are so sinister. The attack on the Bible shows that. Everyone, and I mean every person on this earth, has been merged into this artificial line. Why some are aware and others are not has puzzled me for some time. Is that by design, or just luck? I do not know. It can not be good.

I do not know if Dr. Rose knew of the nefarious plans of the elite, he might not have had a clue. It appears as though he knows this line is being generated and he believes there is some way this time line will be introduced as a separate planet. He can see the ramifications ahead as is indicated by his second prediction. Remember, they were nine years into this when he did his seminar. It is staggering to try and conceive the level these machines are at now. As of this writing they have announced that they have 4069 chips and can access 2 to the four thousandth and something alternate universes! They announce these things, but the sleeping public is unaware. And, thanks to the stigma of being labeled a conspiracy theorist, the aware for the most part stay silent.

None of this means that we are any less real than otherwise. It is just a matter of adjusting particles at the subatomic level. We do that everyday to make this reality. Why can't a machine a few million times more powerful than all of humanity do the same? I don't have the time or inclination to make this a quantum mechanics lesson, just know that on the level they are on they can recreate anything and everything. And they want you to know that and they want you to be shaking in your boots. Screw them!

Dr. Rose tells you that where two of these parallel universes overlap, because of the introduction of the chip into the field of probability, they can reach over and bring back valuable resources into this reality! Now think about that. That is one generation of chip. With this particular chip able to access 2 to the five hundredth power, (that's a number with at least 500 zeros following it), number of parallel universes. They want to tell us where they were technology wise nine years prior and doubling every year up to and including 2008, and will forever from now on. So you try and calculate the number of parallel universes that they can really access. It is much higher than what they will tell you they have. We left the playing field a long time ago. It is fantastic, but it also is the truth.

Here was a puzzle for me. I can see the process of all my timelines, except this one. I see to a point and then it is black. I am really worried about what I can not see. I have connected my heart to my Soul. Therefore I know the information I am processing through the heart is direct from Source through Soul. I can not see other people's time lines. I am wondering if the information being processed by others is from Source any longer, or is it from artificial intelligence?

While talking about seeing, I do not see the energy lines all of the time. However, everything, although still, is shimmering with an energetic glow. It is amazing what the little soul will do when confronted with information processed through one of the fives senses that it does not control. The little soul whistles a little soul tune and slowly walks away like everything is normal. I am mostly in what I call a cosmic blend. I am solid in the third/fourth dimension but in the background the fifth dimension never leaves. It is more being aware of energy than anything else.

When I see someone's energetic body, I can see either two or three bubbles. I know that there is one more but I have not seen that in anyone yet. A baby that has not been downloaded yet is the most beautiful sight I have ever seen. I have been fortunate enough to have been in that particular mode where I can see the light and the truth while holding a one month old girl. All I could see was a bubble of fantastic energy. The energy is different colors within her little energetic body and is very, very active. It is not yet placed at the assemblage point and is free from the beliefs of man. It is a sight to behold. While seeing someone that way, you can not see others, even if they were in a crowd. You can only see one at a time in their infinity. I do not have total control over my internal dialogue as of yet, that is why this seeing energy is off and on right now.

As far as processing knowledge, that has been the most remarkable thing for me. I have to process the knowledge through the *nagual*, because that is where is originates. The information I process daily through my heart is different than this knowledge. So as of now, in order to process knowledge through the *nagual*, I have to do so in dreaming. I can not access the *nagual* all of the time in the waking state. I have some but it was never planned and has always come as a shock.

To access the *nagual* in dreams you have to do more than lucid dreaming. If you dream lucidly and can see yourself, in other words the dream is third person instead of first person; you have been born with a very special gift. That is the hardest thing to do. I spent years looking for my hands in my dreams and once found I would remember to awaken in my dream. You have seen this in the Castaneda books. I had some success and the exercise would lead to lucid dreaming. However what is not taught in those books is that if you are trying to build the dream body into reality, well, you can not do that first person. You have to view the process. I never knew that. I spent years, forty or more, and never considered that. However, I had apparently spent enough focus on the dream state that everything started to click into place.

I have started sleep walking again. I haven't done that since I was a child. This has been going on for three of four months. I had the thought that if I could only use the act of getting out of bed in my sleep as a signal to awaken in my dream it might be handy. I did nothing but had that thought one time. The next time I was sleepwalking and got out of bed, I was aware that I was asleep, I was aware that I was awake in my dream, and I was viewing my body wrapped in energy. Since this has happened, there has been no confusion in my dreams. I am able to recover and process knowledge given in the fifth dimension. I can not bring this knowledge to the wake state unless I process this way. It is however, just as real as this reality.

There is a house that I have gone to in my dreams for as long as I can remember being an adult. I have

104

mentioned this to your mother many, many times. I have described this house to her. I know every room. I have benefited greatly from the vibration of this energetic spot and the entities within. And it amazes me that I have been totally unaware in the tonal. I know that all who are seeking the truth through dreams are being taught on that level. And I am sure everyone's dream teachings are different. I am processing dreams from decades ago and have even started processing things from the peyote experiences that I am amazed I missed.

The fifth dimension is home to the heart of the soul. It is not describable. The one amazing instance I described earlier in this book was the being we know as Earth! We as humans are moving toward the fifth dimension. And the Earth is also. When I was set up to view the spectacular view I described earlier, it was a kind of joke. It was the Earth playing with me. Does that sound fantastic or what? The being we know as Earth is timeless. And, I know that humans and Earth are inseparable. There would not be one without the other. In the fifth dimension we do not live on Earth, we live within the energized body of Earth! This is the highest level that we as the soul dwell with Earth. We move from there. I know that much, but I do not know where we move to.

Personally, this has been the best thing that has ever happened to me. I was fortunately in a position to take advantage of the shift. The shift was my cubic centimeter of chance. I was born with a warrior's heart for freedom. Please don't take that word, warrior, wrong. Our acceptance of that word sometimes depends on the preceding word. Prayer warrior comes to my mind. That is acceptable to society. I use the term in the sense of attitude. I know of no other word that describes that attitude properly. A true warrior is not concerned during battle with the outcome. It is necessary to have this type of attitude because of the impossibility of the feat we are trying to accomplish. This helps develop the proper posture of the heart which is humble gratitude. If you are ever in a position that you do not know what to do, just be humbly grateful. You will never be wrong.

You know all of this. Everyone does in some way. Trust your intuition. What makes you think, People will laugh at me if I go around telling them I am a warrior, is the little soul. The little soul does not want to be laughed at. And why would you want to go around telling everyone something like that anyway? That only adds to self importance, which is what everyone should be trying to decrease.

Self importance is the culprit. Would you like to know where it comes from? Self importance stems from self pity. It is true. When you reach the place of no pity, (there really is a state of consciousness such), you can see these things. The place of no pity does not in any way mean that you are not compassionate towards all of life. It means you no longer feel sorry for yourself or for others. It is such a hoot. Everyone looks like a banty rooster all puffed up and struttin' around with self importance. If at any time in your life you say something offends you, have someone close kick you in the butt! Saying you are offended means you consider yourself too important to be put through the ordeal of hearing or seeing something you do not agree with.

And those that are offended because of their God, well, they are being self important and self righteous. I can not understand the whole kill for my God deal. This world has always been insane. That is what the Cain slaying Able was all about. Brothers are still killing brothers. (Now don't ya'll get any idea!)

The whole Bible, for me, was a book about the expansion of consciousness. That is what Christ Consciousness is. But you will not receive adequate information and teaching in that area in the modern church. It is not the good Christians fault. They are doing the best they know how to do. Churches help an amazing number of people every day. And I am one of those that have been helped. They do everything right and to the best of their ability as far as their understanding goes. And their understanding has been held in place for around seventeen hundred years.

The Nag Hammadi Library is a set of thirteen volumes, or portions thereof, that are called codices. It has appropriately been named The Gnostic Archive. It was dug up in Upper Egypt in 1945. It is an amazing and interesting work to read. While portions of the Gospel of Matthew are among the artifacts, the oldest known Gospel is with these writings also. It is the Gospel of Thomas. It was written in the first century while those of the time of Jesus were still alive.

What is amazing about the Gospel of Thomas is that it is all Gnosticism. Gnostic is simply refusing to accept anything from man or from the external, the *tonal*, and accepting truth only from a personal spiritual event. What happened to Paul on the road to Damascus was a Gnostic event. Jesus was always teaching expanded consciousness, and finding that within. That is all Gnosticism is to me. You have to develop the proper posture in order to receive true knowledge which comes from within.

The early church railed against the Gnostics, wiping them out by the hundreds. The early church did not want the general population knowing anything about consciousness expansion, much less practicing for enlightenment. They ridiculed the Gnostics by accusing them of claiming they had hidden knowledge. The only reason any true knowledge has been hidden is because the church will kill you if you don't.

I have really focused on one thing since 1971. I mean true focus. You may know me as the musician, Roy Horne. Or, you may know me as the business man, Roy Horne. You may know me as the little league or peewee football coach, the neighbor, the Sunday school teacher, the scout leader, the crusader for Christ, your father. All of these and more I did adequately but in none did I excel. Why? My focus was on one thing only. My heart.

You know, and I can not fool you, that I had the intelligence and mental capability to be anything

108

that I wanted to be. So why did I spend all of my twenties and most of my thirties being a musician? The answer is total freedom. I could not even focus on being a better musician during that time. I just wanted to be totally free. Musicians are also naturally bent toward freedom. I enjoy their company. They walk a fine line with reality.

What actually made the Mandela Effect work for me was an actual somersault of thought. Basically, I had spent many years trying to develop the dream body and in so doing make the *nagual*, or dream state, as real and valid as the tonal, or little soul state. There is so much work to be done in some areas that it seems an impossible task. There are ways though.

I mentioned earlier that love is the way. Not so much for dreaming, but for actual transformation through absolute love. But I could not convert and maintain the love vibration. We all experience a lot of static interference. I was more prone to kicking down the door, in a loving way. It is dangerous to do what I was doing. Instead of increasing the validity of the dream reality, I was decreasing the validity of the every day world. Now, my heart has always told me when to stop.

I was sitting out on the back screened porch not too long after I had my transformation. I was looking down at the garden. Suddenly I noticed a large number of small animals the size of armadillos running all around. They were running in a pattern of sorts. It dawned on me that armadillos do not move that fast. As I stood up to investigate, they disappeared. What? I slowly sat back down and they appeared again. I suddenly shifted my perception and noticed a line of ants running in a pattern of sorts on the screen four feet in front of my face! They were very real in the garden, until my perception shifted. They were so real that there was this knowledge within me that I could just let go and I could join their world. But my heart came through loud and clear. You will never come back. I got up out of my chair and slowly went back into the house.

So, as you somewhat know, I have worked on many areas including the internal dialogue, not doing, dreaming, decreasing self-importance, recapitulation and erasing personal history. The recapitulation and erasing personal history really had me hung up for many years. Recapitulation is more than just remembering past thoughts and actions. These actions or thoughts are what the little soul uses to build this matrix we call reality. All of the truth has to first pass through the little soul and all of the baggage of a lifetime. I could erase beliefs. Beliefs are just that, and as such carry no weight at all. But I could not contend with personal history on any level.

The quantum shift did the impossible for me. When I knew, actually knew in my heart, that I had no history on this planet at all, I was amazingly filled with joy. I finally felt free. And that freedom transported me to the absolute truth.

Being in the presence of the Soul is not fearful or even confusing. It is all natural. The mechanics and progression I saw is evident in everything I see now. We each exist on so many levels as well as manifestations. We are always in the fifth dimension. We exist there just as we exist here. There is no space or time.

This whole thing is a manipulation. The elite are now moving toward their New World Order at a blazing pace. If they can create a complete man-made time line, what else do you think they can accomplish? They came online with a quantum computer in 1999, the year of the Columbine incident. Think about it. They did the programming. With all the police shootings and people just pulling guns on the police, could it be all just manipulated. Hard for you to believe? Just look around and your rigid beliefs should be shrinking. They will crash the economy, hope that the work they have been doing for the past few years works and the country will divide by race and fight each other for something to eat. After the desired results have been accomplished they will usher in WWIII. It is not a pretty picture.

Worst of all, the control of quantum computing will for sure make any following reality even more controlled than the Orwellian fascist regime we live in now. But there is light, and that light is truth.

They can do nothing to the man who is working on expanded consciousness. The very act of starting to work on the consciousness lets the little soul know that you are aware of something else and will reach that something in spite of the ranting of the ego. People are too smug and comfortable in their limited knowledge of things. They are not aware, not only of how little they actually know, but they are also unaware that what they think they know is actually a controlled lie to foster control. I can not afford to spend time with the beliefs of men. I can not afford to spend time with any ideology of any kind.

We will be fine, I do not know about the rest of the world. You must focus on and follow your heart, not the mind of men. You have to love everyone. They are just unaware and are playing the lead part of the movie in their head. Just learn to laugh at their endless manipulations.

I love you all dearly. Stay cool. I gotta slide!

September 2016

Made in the USA
Middletown, DE
25 February 2018